As I Write These Words

Samir Georges

iUniverse, Inc.
Bloomington

As I Write These Words

iUniverse books may be ordered through booksellers or by contacting:

iUniverse
1663 Liberty Drive
Bloomington, IN 47403
www.iuniverse.com
1-800-Authors (1-800-288-4677)

ISBN: 978-1-4697-7375-9 (sc)
ISBN: 978-1-4697-7376-6 (e)
ISBN: 978-1-4697-7377-3 (hc)

Printed in the United States of America

iUniverse rev. date: 3/27/2012

For all my readers, old and new; friends and strangers, all family to me. These poems are a collection of feelings and experiences, interpretations and journeys. I write and offer them in the hopes of sharing and, with your permission, inspiring. To my parents and my brother, I offer these poems as a testament to the person you have made me, in thanks for all that you have done.

Introduction

It is in poetry that I find the words to express life, both yours and mine. But when the idea was first proposed to me to publish, it was alien. Most alien of all was the idea that poems I had written for no one could be shared by anyone. I wonder what you will think when you read them; I wonder how you will hear the words that I have never said with my voice. These poems tell of ideas, notions of the heart and mind that are painted with prose and rhyme. Many people have commended the wisdom of my poems, but I have seldom seen it. For me, and mayhap for you, they will always be words of honesty, about themes varied and wide such as ignorance, time, love, loss, and the many questions of life. I do not know if I will ever find the answers to all the questions life has given me, but it is in the subtlety of words well written that I can express the yearning I have within, to answer your questions as well as mine. And so I share with you this book of poems I have written—poems of love and strife, the desire to live, and the angst of death. These are themes old for us all, but oh how they burn new and bright every day when we wonder about them, when life brings us unexpected gifts and curses and we are left to riddle the answers. My truest wish is that you can grow from these poems, that they can help you as they have helped me. Today I share with you my secrets, my answers, the feelings both you and I share—written with a trepid hand that seeks to share answers and riddles, all at once.

Contents

Open Curtains

To a scene of beginning:
Where with a gasp of universal release,
The dark void bursts from the light
Showers worlds with the heat of new passion,
and from darkness comes life.

And so too is born into this world rust
and the dulling of blades,
the birth of habits
when globes dim and dull, glow and growl.

But the emptiness remains vast,
a sight of worldly yearning
Cold to the eyes,
Faint to the touch.

It's a sight caught up in the stars
amidst the ones that have fallen,
the many that are falling still,
and those in our eyes that live.
They remind us
of rolling hills,
the illusion of mountains,
and their promise of clouds;
the uncertainty of faith
and crashing to the earth;
the steady crawl,
the forced ascent;
another promise,
another beginning.

And we rise again, always
in step with the sun,
and the breath of this fuller world
that stands alone all around us,

demanding our hearts and pledge
to live
and begin again; all that once was
to fill this empty space
with something other
than dull yearning
and cold embrace.

And with every word and breath,
a promise
to begin anew.
Rise again as workers tasked
and fill this world with life.

Soft-spoken Words

Softly spoken words arise
from the ashes
in droplets of snow,

and they rise like curtains
shrouding us in cooling shade,
enticing us
with the tingling of their touch.

These heartfelt sensations
that melt away in waves before the sun

leave but a gentle dew
and memories
of soft-spoken words.

– Samir Georges

Wilful Captive

I'm sitting in the perfect place,
feeling very present
from the ebbing of the pain in my ankle,
the tickle I feel upon my brow,
the fading ache of the bench against my back,
and the ease of every breath,
to the touching of the wind
like a gentle rain that leaves no mark behind,
to the pleasantness of the bird mere struts away,
to the ant intruding on my thoughts
and the smoothness of the water trickling
so close to my ears.

Even the pavement beneath my clothed feet
feels soft yet unyielding.
The fly that twirls around
and the clearness of my eye—
Oh, I am caught in a perfect place
between two worlds.

Whispers

The flash of a bulb.
"Sorry" flashes
in my mind.
Echo.

The pulse of my mind,
snap of the camera.
  Snap!
Echo.
  Sorry.

Pregnant rain
slushes down the sky,
Lightning skidding
through the drops.
  Snap.
Fading flash ploughs
back to the camera,
  my mind.

Clouds limp past, dragging.
Sorry, I can no longer hear the
  whisper.
Snap, flash, all gone, huddled
in a ball in the back of
my mind.

A drop,
another,
jolt my sleeping senses.
A swarm, rain rails down, cold.
A startled cry—
  they awake.
Shredding the wind,
clouds streak by; steam engines, like flashes, burn my eyes.

– *Samir Georges*

The sun blazes upward; I crane my neck
to catch it—too fast,
gone,
the whisper
      gone.

A Foul Business

In debt to this world,
Silent is she
Who is spared no sympathy.
Stripped of her fruitfulness,
Once so welcoming and whole,
Now she lays there,
Her pride an open door.
A crippled beast once wild
Discarded there, unspoken,
To be picked at by carrion
Or mauled at by those remorseless needs.

One day a dear friend came by to include
His hungering smile,
Putting no effort to hide
His green teeth, a gleaming pride.

– Samir Georges

Whirlpool of Fate, Siren Grasp of Quicksand

Swallowed by your path, Panic!
Wriggling in its strong grasp, Suffering!
Subdued beneath its murk, Frantic!
Twitching weakly with hope, Flickering …!

Peacefully captive bound soul, Unspoken …
Recalling events long past, Ebbing …
Neglected feelings swirl out, Broken …

Motivated

It's the flight of pregnant birds that I am reminded of:
Bloated and cramping,
Legs tucked close in, wings beating away with paternal efficacy,
Never toward a nest,
Always in flight,
As if the very notion of rest—a circling falcon,
A tireless hunter—promising a swift demise
and the loss of pregnant life.

This, this is a pregnant flock of desires and ideas,
Notions and purpose,
Encumbered and floating, rolling clouds laden with rain.
And this flock rolls on,
Until with a spasm of wings and anticipated rhythm;
A gush of rains and new life is announced
And from each bird, pregnant from birth,
Comes a new flock, each and every belly swollen with life.
And new ideas surge forth,
And newly feathered wings beat with renewed zeal,
And a multitude of pregnant flocks take to the skies.

And it's these birds I'm reminded of
When I pick up the pen to write,
Because in each and every bird I observe,
I see that pregnant mother of possibility
Beating her wings, soaring above the ground
To give birth in the skies,
Where my ideas soar, soar, and give birth.
And I am reminded of them
Every time I come to write
And fear I will write nothing at all.

– *Samir Georges*

Misdirected

I'd say I love you, but that could change.
I'd say I hate you, but that would change.
I'd say a million words if only they could fix us.
I'd call you beautiful,
I'd call you an angel.
I'd speak of your eyes like they were pearls in the deep ocean—
But that would do no good.

I'd give you my heart,
My never dying love.
I'd give you my mind;
I gave you my dreams.
My hopes linger around your footsteps,
And I flinch when you hurt,
I cry when you mourn,
I falter when you suffer,
I lie by your moon as you sleep,
I gaze at you till fatigue takes me away.
Then as I dream you fill my heart.
I'd give you my soul,
But of no value it is to you.
But I could give you my love;
I think I shall.

Tonight, the mirror broke;
A thousand pieces lie before me.
It shattered as you dropped my rose,
The rose that wilted in your hand.
My heart shrivelled in my chest,
My soul crumbled in my shell.
The drop of a tear echoes like a mourner's bell
As you went to another.
You have stolen my heart,
You have stolen my mind,
You have stolen my dreams,

Wasted my words, my time.
You have misdirected the glow of the moon so that its beauty was lost to me.
Now you leave, and the world heaves a sigh.
"Rest now," says the moon,
"For tomorrow you shall meet the sun."

– *Samir Georges*

More than Once I Beckoned

More than once I beckoned,
More than once I tried
To cower down beneath you,
My shadow, my pride.

Remembering Pictures

Snap
    of the camera.
Crashing
down, comes the
flash!
Memories like pictures,
brilliant white tulips
blossom
in my mind.
Yawn, open,
gaping for my sight.
Snap,
echoes,
the blossoming tulip
melts,
a little sun that
winks, once, twice, out.

I'm in a dark room.
The flash,
only an echo,
sinks
down into memories
like droplets of
pregnant rain,
slushes down my
breath.
    I
cough.

Snap.

Blazing
globe surges up,
flares,

– Samir Georges

washes away the rain,
rages into my mind
A blinding light,
snap.
A tulip flowers,
the echo begins
and, as always,
melts away.

And the
rain comes
crashing down.
Startled senses wake,
startled emotions real.
A startled me
remembers
pictures.

The Monster without Purpose

A mountain of grounded rock reaching to the skies,
A rabbit burying into a hole,
A pig building a house of straw—
Why, concrete little pig, brick and sweat.
A tree, untrimmed and ungainly;
Buzzing insects, foaming with diseases and the chance of death
All around a mound of sand,
A sand castle,
A poor sign of engineering
Yet fit for a queen.
Build straight pathways, not curving halls, little ant;
Your purpose is there, it's your efficiency that lacks.
Take note from the concrete, the velvet and the vibrating,
The ironman working the ironworks in the iron mine—
Purpose, purpose, purpose.
He earns his iron dollar,
They raise their iron children,
Time rusts their flawed, iron hearts.
The silver-tongued king rules his copper-minded people,
The golden patience of time rules the silver-tongued king,
The velvet soft lover wrestles with the friction of passion.
The ninety-nine-year-old man is killed for his crimes.
The copper-minded populace cheers;
Some shed fake diamond tears,
And we spin our web of lies,
Our empire of cobwebs, time-formed truths
Threatened by the subtle breeze of our patient host,
True diamond patience of Earth.

So the philosopher asks
Riddles with himself.
Earth has no purpose but to be,
And to be without purpose is not our way,
Yet we unfurl our carpet in its chambers of torrents
And build our houses of straw

– *Samir Georges*

And build our mountains of steel.
And we expect to persevere,
So this purposeless world,
Moulded of chance and mutation,
It sits by, without reasons to impede;
It sits by, as time hammers at its walls.
A purposeless measure, the ticking of a clock;
The clock ticks, yet the batteries have long passed,
The maker long gone.
Still we build; a raging force in the calm of chaos,
And the solidarity of this fortress called earth,
The permanence of its chaos,
Is challenged by a rusting blade.
The blade rises against the mountain
and with precise slashes,
chips away at the uneven granite.

The blade chips, the dead clock ticks,
The mountain sits.

A Quest Within

My green gaze befalls
The sceptre.

It floats on a pedestal,
    Hums a tune soft to my ears.
The glow, beacon, scampers toward me,
    Tugs at my leg.
I plow forward through my stubborn reservations.
    Walls, barriers, built before;
Another's toil.
    I pummel through,
Mighty to rubble, my toil.
    I scuttle back down the hall,
A dull orange rod in my sweaty palm.

I brush away the dust,
Weave my way through my greatest art,
Meeting no resistance.

    Grim—
A gated barrier around my heart,
And behind quivers my joy.
I beat away the steel,
Sceptre on rock,
Dull and dented rod on a mountain,
Resistance.

– Samir Georges

We Await Her Arrival

Our maiden of secrecy,
Cherished by the stars,
Whored by the moon—
We wait for her day and night.

Our hearts flutter into specs of cherished dust
As they escape from us in every cherished breath;
As they embrace us once more, we draw them back in.

This sensation that stings our eyes,
Draws our lids, draws our sight,
Draws our thoughts
Inwardly, as we fall back upon a cloud mattress—
It embraces us, envelops us from within.
She who inspires each breath,
We wait for her in every wisp of night air,
With every breath we let stray.
Our hearts are rebuilt of hope,
Hope that she would come.
Carried aloft our very needs
To meet us upon our cushion of clouds,
And with every breath we retake,
Hope is shattered.
But as quickly as it is gone,
As surely as our next breath,
As surely our very next moment,
Hope returns.

We fall in trance.
Our maiden, hidden in her caves.
Drunken sleep takes her away.
The world our maker
Whisks her into his forays.
The swirling dusk, a grey breeze in the darkness—
We are left behind, in the dark.

Our desperate eyes cling to the distance;
A spotlight speaks to our sight.
She is around the corner, it says.
This want from within
Inspires each breath. As we race to meet the light,
As it inches ever away, we pound through the dark,
Panting, and we collide into her.
In a burst of cool night air,
We close our eyes.
She is there,
Within.
Our minds can picture nothing else, our eyes smile,
Our lips quiver
With every breath.

– Samir Georges

Sand Castle

As my country was bombed and I was lifted away into the skies,
I looked back and promised myself
I would not forget this house of sand in these times of rain.

She Was the Proudest of Birds

Her nest was made of woven gold, silver embroidery;
Her two little eggs polished to reflect the mother's loving smile;
And guardian over this lavish nest, a warrior bird with talons and zeal.

But she was proudest most of her plume
Wild and extravagant, rich red speckles over deep hazel feathers,
Their edges like the hems of a dress, entwined with brilliant white.

But the envious world set an eagle to take her plumage,
And her husband dove with him to the skies, and there they battle still.
In desperation they sent a winged fox to slip through the clouds,
and the sly demon came on winds of ill will and ruined her nest,
Took hostage her eggs.

Humbled, she shed her plumage, scattered it for the world to hoard—
All the price for these little eggs with fickle shells to be returned.
And naked without husband, she looked down upon their plain shells,
And reflected there, a mother's loving smile.

– *Samir Georges*

Stars

One amongst the multitude would gaze up in awe,
And in his sight he would capture
A moment as unique as it is common:

A hovering globe,

Overflowing with gold, showering the multitude with brilliant currents,
Mother to the rivers of El Dorado.
And each droplet would sink into the soil beneath,
Birthing glimmering auric trees from each seedling shed.
And so did more of the multitude come to gather;
The mulling throng stood dazed and gazing,
Mesmerized by the omniscient presence looming above.

Until one day,
One by one,
The multitude became few and the few became none,
Receding to the ground.
And one by one did the none become many,
And grow did a multitude of shimmering sprouts,
Till one day did appear a clustered forest
Swaying to and fro in the healthy breeze
In tribute to the sphere of imminence above,
Swinging more frantically in the anticipating gust.
But with glooming realization
Did they notice
    A fading orb.

And the leaves rustled their protests;
With heart-aching comprehension, the trees stretched themselves,
But only could they stare, limbs strained, as their sun faded away
And found its long awaited place amongst companions,
Stars in our distant past.

Night-time

I love the feeling of the night-time,
When the sun is drowned in the dark,
And I can dip my feather in this sea of ink
And on paper soar.

– *Samir Georges*

Love and Loathing

I love holding you in my arms,
Bodies entwined,
Breathing of life and contentment
Together.

And as I hold you in my arms,
I loathe
That all my mind can do,
Weak in the thrall of content,
Is hold you some more.

The Philosopher

He pushes aside the weathered curtain,
The colourless tub, the bland tiles, his grey glazed sight.
He looks over his shoulder and invites her into his mental fortress.
The king philosopher's decreed writer
To write his thoughts as they rise
Forth from the ashes of the furnace in his mind,
Invisible phoenixes, a wonder never seen.
The writer is a woman, beautiful; his fantasies rule with an iron hammer.
He feels nothing for the imaginary woman;
His dreams told of respect, of falling in love in its truest form:
The caesarean of his mind,
And she would fall in love with the thought burning society within.

So she sat there, somewhere, laptop in hand.

The philosopher closes the curtain, undresses; the water is warm,
It caresses him like no lover ever has.
This water that stirs the slumbering giant within his flesh
Unlocks the rusting, fading iron gate within.
He closes his fragmented eyes;
The distorted images disappear, and his mind kisses aching wounds.
He sighs.
In his mind she waits behind the curtain; it must be awkward.
He does not smile, but his lips part, and he sighs the heat away.
The water cools,
The philosopher sits.
The small tub is a tight fit; he looks down,
The flaws of man so bare before him.
He sees them in many a light,
Riddled with protruding edges of perception;
He tucks his fragmented eyes away.
The philosopher looks down on the folds of his flesh again—
The hair, the child of nature and god, an unholy affair.
His hand runs over his thigh, the meaningless hair, the soft fat.

– Samir Georges

His fragmented eyes see the flaws of society,
A misguided shamble of enterprises, the idea of destiny a delusion.
His misty eyes see a cripple.

He dictates his poem,
She writes.
He looks up at the curtain, the veil separating him from humility,
And he sees its transparency.
He sees the inadequacy of definition,
Of documenting his emotion and the ideas of his furnace.
He realizes the chaos of his being.
He looks down again,
He sees a handsome man:
Thin, fit, comfortably sitting in the tub.
Society in acceptance of itself and the reality of its situation,
And behind that lie, he still sees a cripple.

He draws the curtain open,
His weary legs haul him over gravity's threshold.
He sways, the water leaving through the drain with the rest of his will,
his strength.
He steps past his mind's mistress
And crumples onto the floor
Gracefully, like an empty shirt folding down upon itself.
His mind lies, his knees hurt.
The cold tiles send shivers across his body;
He begs for the heat, the sapping warmth.
The penetrating cold reinvigorates its assault—
No mercy for the wicked, the weak.

Again he realizes how inadequate words are.
The cold to him is like the slap of a parent;
The sting left behind is the memory of failure,
The warmth to him is like the lull of a siren,
The dulled senses are the reward of failure.

The writer draws the curtains on her pity-stained eyes

And looks away; her job is to write, but here she has to endure his pain.
She reaches out a tentative hand, blind to his turmoil,
Speaks her words; they wash over him like a comforting breeze.
The breeze envelopes him like the hug of a thorn bush;
His wet body shivers.
She looks at his casing, lumped against the tiles,
Flesh seeking escape through pores within ceramic.

He drapes his eyelids over his archaic eyes,
His fragmented eyes reflect the light inward,
His gluttonous eyelids hoarding his secrets away from the world.
But he can still see; he cannot tell, but he can see
The raging torrents within this house of flesh,
The denizens of his crumbling fortress,
The smoke of the furnace suffocating them—always
They seek a full lung, unclouded air,
Enough to satisfy every pore of his tired body.
He sighs, an attempt to seduce the turmoil, a silent question.
The chaos abides; his eyelids drag their mass upward.

And so his fragmented eyes look away.
The furnace of his mind hires mindless drones.
He drapes a towel over his cold folds;
His lady rubs the seams of her skirt,
Closes her laptop,
And his reality locks the rusting iron gates within shut,
The smoke of the furnace churning for release.
He dries himself,
Walks over to his room, the cold touching him in unwelcome places.
He puts on his layers of fabrics over the folds of his flesh;
Beneath them the iron gates help the world pretend,
Pretend that the words are wolves with fangs,
That the turmoil is held at bay.
But the presence of the iron gates, the warm clothes,
the seductive words, do not lie.

– *Samir Georges*

The philosopher shoulders his burden and prays the next shower will be more merciful.
The philosopher shoulders his burden and pretends that his shrivelled form can brace the weight.

He Whistles as He Walks, This Man

He whistles as he walks,
This man who knows not love,
And he comes upon a sea
Where upon the other side is the wanting bosom of the horizon.
But this man he cannot cross the torrents,
For this man he knows not love.
So he walks along the coast and comes upon a lighthouse;
It shines its light across the wide expanse of blue,
Screaming out with its bright blinding light,
"Here! I call you, star-crossed lovers, here!"
And he is blind to its call; he sees an abandoned shell,
This man who knows not love.

He whistles as he walks,
This man who knows not love,
And he comes upon a child and her favourite memory,
Nestled in the arms of her long-lost father,
Gazing dreamily at the lapping waves.
And he walks through these haunting spectres,
For they are naught for this man who knows not love,
And he whistles as he walks
But hears no tune.

– *Samir Georges*

Sleepily

The father visits his son in the dark of day;
The son is abed, pale in the light of night,
For the sun and moon are witnesses in this hour of twilight,
But the sun is not heat and does not shine as bright,
And the moon is not rigid rock.
The sun is a warm hope, fading ever so slightly;
The moon is softness, the dark soothing.

The son is abed, covers sprawled over his listless form;
The son is restless, he does not sleep;
The son is ebbing, his heart does weep.
And his father lifts the covers up tight around his chest
And kisses his brow.
The son blinks wearily, smiles wanly, whimpers meekly.

"Sleep, my son," the father whispers.

"But I cannot sleep." Sleep eludes him.
"I want to play." Rest prances about him,
Close enough to want, just out of reach.
"And how can I sleep, Father?" How can he rest atop this fated bed,
When he wishes to wake, when his heart does weep restlessly?

The father wavers; he caresses the son's brow, but not his heart,
For the heart is within, the caress without—
The eternal divide.
"Rest, my son," he says, "rest and forget."

"But Father, Father, why?
My heart will not sleep.
Five more minutes? Just five."

"Sleep, son, the hour is late, the time is nigh."

And the father, always lovingly, pulls the covers tight over the son

And lowers him into hallow ground.

And so comes death,
Deaf to all that is within,
Cold to all that stands without,
And all mothers and fathers are but witness.

– *Samir Georges*

Alone We Are Resolute

Alone we are resolute
in the stand we take
when we live these moments
as but moments,
with no tale to drag
or future to unfold.

We resign ourselves
when we string the bow before we loose
and choose the arrow before the quarrel;
string the bow before we loose,
place that arrow before we forget
all that is around us, in this moment;
drag our breath before we aim,
sight our target;
and breathe before we launch,
launch this moment into the next.

It is then that we feel joy
in the moment before release,
and resign ourselves
in the resoluteness of these moments
that beg our world pause
to live.

Remnant

There lay a bear, his swaying fur, his blank stare,
Down by my feet,
Which have seen no dryness or showering sun.
This remnant,
This shade of a carcass,
That looming presence of a fading power,
Paws tucked away beneath his shadow;
A place for all your troubles,
This world's misery—
All engulfed within his husky prestige
And beneath his smothering roar.

This fur
By my feet,
Aside my shadow,
The fire calms it with tender caresses
As it mourns its loss.
This fur, an echo of a behemoth's greatness—
His blood-drenched paws,
His bellowing roar,
His guilty eyes,
His steady shoulders—
'Tis lost to us
In the fire's hue.

– *Samir Georges*

Shoulder

My shoulder has drowned away and died,
Yet another awaits your storms.

Grim

Touch my hand;
I will not speak.
Don't take that step;
I will not peek.
Don't hold your breath;
There is no cause,
But that of my love.
Strife,
The loss of a life.
Step back,
Don't take it,
Don't take a leap
Of faith or lack thereof.
The road ends here;
There lies a cliff, below resides the Grim;
Call out as you drift into the dim.
Look at me and tell if you see him, that Grim.
Lift your chin high,
Show him nothing but your determination,
Show him your silhouette as you walk back into my sunlight.
Arch your gold-flecked wings;
Let him, that darkness that haunts your footsteps, writhe in jealousy.
Make this step be heard,
Leave a track of broken hearts and shattered dreams,
Be the cause and not the excuse.
You're not lost, you are found;
You're not loved, you are dreamt;
You're not hated, you are unnoticed.
Don't see him smile—he isn't there,
That grim that you carry.
Share it with me; I can take a burden.
My words will weave a bottomless basket for your distress.
Share a smile, maybe a laugh, share a sign, maybe be kiss.
Give me that basket,
Carry this heart,

– *Samir Georges*

Hide it, it's yours.

Don't take that step;
Touch my hand.
I promise I'm not him,
That Grim.

These Words Are Liberty

The words are liberty—
the liberty I've always craved,
the liberty of freedom, as limited as words may be,
as limited as the breath of life may be.

Oh I wish to fly into Tokyo,
on top of winds that weave with an artist's hand
and to the soft-spoken haiku whispered in my ear;
oh with the liberty of words.

I can share a moment, gift an eternity,
and have you hold my hand
all the way into Tokyo,
all blinking lights and reaching peaks,
as we land into Tokyo
hand in hand on the whims of poetry.

– Samir Georges

Content

A behemoth of fire and rage,
Red scales glimmering with deadly potency.
Its absurd cries of evil shatter empires;
Its unjust breath of malice devours lives.

So comes forth a shining knight,
A star descended from the heavens,
An answered wish to the denizens of mankind,
And with a sword gleaming altruism,
He cuts down the dragon, and rightfully so.

And just reward does follow this magnanimous deed;
Maidens and praise and—
A fated car horn.

I awake
And, with the reflexes of a knight,
Catch my book as it slips my grip.

Smiling, I find my page
Just as the not-so-chivalrous knight
Slew the not-so-fearsome dragon,
And if for moments more
I live on as a knight,
Content with well-worn pages
If not maidens and praise.

I Am Captain

I am captain
of a ship,

but my ship, it is living
with flesh and blood,
with flooding veins
and drowning organs.

I am captain
of a living ship,

but my ship, it is falling
down from the highest harbour,
down between sea and sky
into the dead horizon below.

I am captain
of a falling ship,
of a sinking ship,
and day by day
it sinks deeper
into the horizon.

– Samir Georges

Race Way

On a race way by a mirage,
Zoom past the scenery:
A beautiful meadow,
Spring rich in its blossoms.
Race past as you are caught up in a whirlwind,
'Round and 'round,
Past beauty,
Past the beast,
Past your world,
Your short-lived breath.
Leave them all behind as your memory clears away,
Caught up in this race as it all slips by.

So jump,

Jump away and embrace this mirage;
It might be real
And lose you the race,
But find out for yourself, live before you die.
This mirage we've created,
This haven we've forgotten,
Abandoned—
Time wraps its tail around our necks and squeezes;
Constrict it might, our final breath unspent.
This constricting python, a devil in its own.

Just sit down upon this wasteland
And dream yourself into heaven,
The heaven we let slip as time takes over.
Break away from reality,
Let your breath slip away noticed,
Let every heartbeat be heard
Fill your eyes with beauty,
Let the beast be bathed in tranquil waters.
No levels to these plains, no chins lowered or raised,

All level with this paradise we so crave, yet so deprived.
Let a kiss last forever and bear the breath of life;
Let your emotion decide the outcome,
Free from the corruption of your thought;
Lie upon a mattress of life, embrace the calling,
Each breath well spent.

Ready yourself with an inhale, your breath to be lost once more.
Close your eyes and imagine that hell,
Open arms march forward,
Chin raised, chest pumped, heart pounding, feet stamping.
And let your cry be heard,
Enter that track and lead the race,
For time shall not wait,
And only death is so patient.

– *Samir Georges*

Glistening White

Throwing back the sunlight
in mouthfuls of white,
trying to flood the universe
with his finite cheer,
all there reflected in a smile.

Little feet scurry around,
little hands wave up and down
seeking, finding
a world ready and welcoming.
The air they breathe, the wind they feel
laughs on all around them,
livid in their joy.
It tickles them when they trip,
and they always rise back again,
they always want to run again,
they never think they'd fall again,
and the air cheers on all around them.
Oh, and when they cry,
tears fall down and shatter against the earth,
unwelcome but excused.

And when the air laughs no more,
and the wind is sullen and forlorn,
you know the mist has begun its crawl,
white as glistening teeth
rugged, with age-worn eyes and a gnarled touch,
inhaling all the familiar warmth,
breathing out air stale with cold.
And while the mist lingers,
this garden wilts and decays,
and in the shade of fog grow weeds and thorns
rising to trip and prick.
And lo the wind can stand by no more;
it bellows through the mist, soars down to defend its charge,

and turns out of the haze a haunted demon,
twisted and lost,
battering those smiles with hail and rain.
It roars them to tears, tears of fright and loss.
The earth shuts its doors in futility;
little feet pound down in frustration,
little hands grow claws and scratch back.

They shut out the sunlight on this garden
and grimace
into the murky dark.

– Samir Georges

Where I Was

I was arriving home one night,
the smell of smoke clinging to my shirt,
the laughs at the café humming around my ears,

and I looked up at that sky—
such a homely shade of grey,
but my gaze kept climbing and straining,
picks in hand, climbing over and over,
oh so draining,
till all was stayed by a concrete behemoth,
when on all three sides of my limited vision
all I saw was wall.

My heart scrambled for release,
and I forced my eyes against the dread.
Up, and up, rolling up, gravity clinging on; still I looked,
and all I saw was wall,
all kinds of painted wall.

Red, orange, brown, and grey.
Grey skies,
my eyes guzzling in the greyness
like starved infants at their mother's teat.
My heart slowed; the hum of the café carried past in the breeze,
Echoes of laughter
across grey skies.

I must have been as far away from Earth
as I could ever be,
while standing there on that street,
feeling so very detached.

Till the moment that some unnamed flock of white bird
came charging through from distant worlds,
streaking across grey skies.

And just at that very same moment, squinting,
drinking in the white mass of life, fleeing my stare
on that dark, humid night,
with the echo of laughter still in the air, clinging to my shirt,
muddled in smoke
choking my sense of belonging,
I knew exactly
Where I was.

– Samir Georges

Dreamer

I'm a happy dreamer.
I am that cocooned butterfly
In a shell of fragile webs,
That dreams of flying, a splitting of the cage,
Oblivious to the outside
Where stretches a spider's net
Neatly waiting,
Oblivious to my dreams.
Oh, happy dreams.

I Shall Find You

Running,
Running so fast.
I think the time has passed.
Today has lost its track.
If I am not there by today,
Tomorrow is just a mile away.

Running so fast,
I can't seem to find
The end to this track.
I've lost my senses—
My eyes,
My ears,
My taste,
My touch,
My smell.
My love for you drowns them out.
I run blindly toward a light I do not see,
But it is you I look for;
Today or tomorrow,
I shall find you.
Wanting I am of your touch,
Of your gaze,
Your taste of my loves and hates,
Your listening to my needs,
The smell of your breath upon my face.
I run to you, in a circle I have passed a thousand times before.
There you are, just past that horizon,
Like the one before, a million times before.
I think I'll rest, just for a little.
Today or tomorrow,
I shall find you.

– *Samir Georges*

Cherish Your Pockets

Crimson king of freedom,
Wise men fill your coffers with gold,
Decorate your crucifixion with diamonds.
The sight of sacrifice ordained with sin,
Vanity raging rampant.

He Built Another Planet

Perched upon a behemoth,
a mountain, a companion to a lonely god—
perched is a man
who eyes the ground,
his captivating obsession.

He saw the land change with beautiful colours:
green landscapes would burn bright red
and pave the path for great grey masses,
come to overrule all colour,
come to embroider the earth below.
Rise and fall would these structures, spread and flow,
like the flowing of water amongst the rapids.
And from his divine perch he admired
the flow of the land, and the peoples therein.

One day, his urge overwhelmed him, as only urges do,
and the mountain was patient, as only mountains are.
He departed to the depths,
whereupon landing with feet wearily planted,
the pain of urges was known to a god.

It was the world he so admired—
no blurred painting of majestic colours.
Blue streaks memory convinced him were rivers
became the swollen tears of mountains.
Green earth he once greedily lavished with his gaze
now repulsed him; a brown earth died green with greed and folly.
Ruins scarring the dead land,
So flawless from far,
Yet so riddled with questions and doubts when near.

So again his urge overwhelmed him to return,
and perched by his companion, he would say,
"I think I am content by your side,
taking note from a mountain, content
to leave my urges be."

– *Samir Georges*

Never Ending

I was so careless.

You try so hard,
You strive so blindly,
Your will of strife
Lost in reality.

I think I'd better leave,
Lie to you and to myself.
Please answer my cries,
Those silent cries,
Those cries that beg me speak;
Answer them before in silence I depart.

Can I gaze into your eyes and fall into my coffin with a smile?
Those beautiful eyes, crystal yet so murky,
Deep in obscurity.
Can I gaze at my dreams and welcome my loss,
Or shall you answer these cries?

I offered my words;
You gave them back as whispers.
I offered my ears, the joy of sound,
and now you rob me of your voice.
Can I have a nod?
Maybe a kiss good-bye,
A moment?

I guess I'd better leave.
I'm leaving my heart behind,
I'm leaving my reckless heart,
I'm leaving my yearning eyes,
My careless self behind.

Fathom

Night and day
A tug and pull of lovers never entwined.
Beauty and force,
The caress and the crave.
As the sun fades beneath the dawn
And the light slowly retreats,
The night, edging forward,
Seeking to touch, to grasp—
But too late, as the light fades away:

And it is here,
the darkness has settled.
The dark is omnipresent,
A depth of universe
So vast, so full of stars and worlds,
So enshrouding, a blanket of secrets and untold deeds
So grand and great,
So mighty, unquestionable,
Inevitable,
For the dark to encroach, encompass and overwhelm.

This night,
It stands all around us
With no peers or equals.
The light long gone, long faded,
And the night, it waits till the fawning of the sun,
The first sign of light
To fade away,
Alone, every night
In its grandeur,
Alone.

– *Samir Georges*

A World of Vintage Leather

Politicians on monkey bars,
Politicians in presidential cabinets,
The blind a common sight to see.
Rise, I say.
Shout, I pray.
March, damn you and your willingness
To sit by,
To watch behind TV screens and bomb shelters.
But wait—

"Hope, come to me."
I call you, hope; come to me, come to us,
Lead us, for can we lead ourselves?
Yes, no—
Too complicated is this world.
Let's indulge in fabricated lies and drinks.
Drink out of your pint of home-brewed conspiracies;
Don't let it spread
To your children.
Don't pass on this gene;
Let it not be heritable,
Or are we so afflicted,
So afflicted,
We can't?

No, yes—
If we can, rise up, defend
Our right to be righteous,
Our right to attack
Those who condemn our righteousness.
They label, they bottle you up with lies.
Hey, ho!
I say,
Can you say
What I say?

Together, side by side.
Divided, we beg them conquer;
United, we defy the monger.
It boils,
It rumbles,
The quake that shakes the horizon.
"Come one,
Come two,
Come all!"
Take all those in your stride and rise, together!
Let the people share the same beat,
The rhythm in your blood,
The one of people,
Of liberty,
Of nations in peace,
The death of greed—
But not while your sons are gone,
Not when your sons are blind;
They need guidance.
Open their eyes, oh mother of fortune.
Mother!
Open your children's eyes,
Crusted and worn.
Let them dance,
Dance to the rhythm of your womb,
And give birth to a new generation
Untainted by the sickness,
To sit by while others flounder.
I can see,
But I feel blind.
Where I walk, so few follow;
Where you beckon, so few notice.
There they tread
To the dead horizon, with its drunken sun and hung-over moon,
Its twisted ways,
Its backward path into greed and misfortune:
Where sitting by the screen of the world,

– *Samir Georges*

Where none can reach you
And you can reach none,
Where free people accept lives of deprivation.
Here we are
In witness to our crimes,
In deep contemplation
Whether to rebel
Or suffer deprivation.

Hey ho, I say no!
My legs will carry me,
And my arms will carry those without legs,
And my eyes,
My eyes
Will see
My mother,
Who
Beckons
Her children,
Beckons
Our youth,
The future
To the quaking horizon,
To the rumbling,
Tumbling,
Mumbling
Blind man's destination,
To where so few tread.

Breathe,
Focus,
Consider.
Will we consider?
Will we?
Will we
See:
The horizon, it quakes

No more,
Its goal fulfilled.
We see, we see what needs to be seen, what quaked to be seen.
We see the future in danger,
We see our forsaken horizon.
Come on!
I say
Break the screen,
Jump into the world,
Rise up and say,
Forsaken mother,
We
See
You.

Let none deny
The privilege we are born to.
Let none beckon
Our rights to the slums.
The horizon has worked.
Drum
Beat.
None so obsolete
As those who cry,
Then lie in tears
Of last night's misery.
We will swim
Through seas and oceans of tears, and walk out
Dry with righteousness by our sides,
And a flaming horizon
Beckoning.

– *Samir Georges*

The Final Tune of the Tick Tock Clock

If I had just one day to live,
Twenty-four hours to feel complete,
Would I race across the castle of my dreams,
Hunted by the echo of the tick tock clock,
Dreading the moment that fateful tune came to a halt,
Chasing down runaway thoughts,
Frantically piecing together broken promises—
All while fearing the silence, the end of the tick, tock?

Rather
I would gaze up at the steps of this sky-high castle,
This floating montage of my life,
And lounge upon the first step,
Resigned to enjoy these fated moments
Without fear or regret,
Resigned to enjoy this melody with those I love,
This farewell tune played to me by the tick tock clock.

One Hall Too Many

tell me otherwise:
speak to me words
that betray your departure.
oh, these halls do not miss the silence
before the echo of our voices.

it is true that stars—
as grand as they are, beacons in space—
true, that stars die,
and oh the star you planted in my heart,
with the speaking of your name,
longs for kindling.

and your smile,
oh, the edges of your smile,
are the tips of the puppeteers strings
that make my soul dance.

these nights feed an addiction to us.
these days bring the sun to us.
these lies set the storms on us.

So lost.

another wasted lie,
another wasted breath,
another wasted thought.
your words leave me here unnoticed;
I cry out as you leave without notice,
and in silence I appreciate the loss,
that I'm right here
where you left me,
amidst a storm of lies and cries and yells and screams and tears
shed for a reason lost in anger.
another wasted kiss.

– *Samir Georges*

another wasted tear—
again they go unnoticed;
these halls cry silence once more.

and do we make of love
nothing but a tear shed and wiped away,
discarded with the rest of our past?
you, a future I have lost,
awash on a beach of floods and storms.

ah, the pillars have begun to show their wear,
and there is no sound in this hall
but silence.
as tears befall a beaten soul and a deserted hall,
this is
Farewell.

Grand

Death is so grand,
So unfathomable;
And my life so small,
Like the shadow before the encroaching dark,
The grand depth of the universe.
And come night,
The shadow is gone.

– *Samir Georges*

Judgment

Judgment,
it is not as difficult
as the dawning of the sun,
nor as complex as rain
on a clouded day.

far more like
the joy of apples
to the hungry,
or treading water
in the sea,
is this sand-drenched tongue
that laps up every morsel of wetness
    from my hand.
this tongue that so passes judgment
    on me,
like the rhythmic need
of a frozen dancer,
is the passing of judgment
in every breath you take
before every one of mine.

Beneath the Rubble of a Once Majestic Tyrant

There are tyrants
far and wide,
and wherever they may be, it is their way to loom.

This tyrant, it loomed with all the gloom of cement,
towered with all the might of concrete
that once loomed over his servants in quiet contemplation.
And when foundations quaked, and the dust was unsettled,
came tumbling down this tyrant, and where tyrants go
servants follow,
and to his fate he took, as he crumbled,
many a servant.

Beneath the rubble, these resonating remnants
still struggled, one more servant
fighting and defying his master's beckoning calls.

"Come to me, crimson child, drenched in the light of the setting sun.
Fall to me, succumb to the twists of creation,
their firm grasp around you. Why resist so?"
This pestering would persist, and this child would struggle,
struggle under the tons of rubble.
With each push of struggle came a gush of crimson,
till the depth of this pool would be too hard to resist.
Yet resist he would,
for this child knew one more push would mean freedom,
one more push would throw away all this rubble,
launch it into the endless space
up above, launch it where dreams slumbered and wept
up above, where the world was weightless.
He would defy gravity with sheer will.

Or was it will? Was it the need to survive,
or was it the want to survive,
the damning desperation to live?

– *Samir Georges*

The sheer desperation, the full loss of control,
Where the mind would take that crimson hand,
make of it a harbinger of good,
crimson for blood, life, hope,
the hope that somehow this crimson child may remain a child
and not lose childhood to cement.
Live, this hand says,
live for eons to come,
soar above the rubble,
whisk through fields of dreams.

Let your mind burst open in a spurt of irrationality.
Let your heart beat to the thrum of life
as your blood dances along,
your mind relishing this dream of ecstasy.
Your body will convulse, throwing your jaw open,
and your mouth will release a roar so fierce,
reality would bow, the rubble no more.
Yet those rocks choose to crush down.
His jaw lets out the silence of a final breath.
Your body will stiffen; telling the child that all would be all right,
all would end soon.
The mind can only offer toys and tricks,
like only cheap tricksters can.
The blood will march, head down and shoulders slumped.
The heart will play a tune of mourning and sadness,
wailing as mothers do against the madness
of a world as mad as only real worlds can be.

Dreams will wilt and wither,
and life ends as hope fades away,
up into the land of distant dreams,
a fading victim
in the reality of cement
and concrete.

Theme of Birds

On the theme of birds that flutter and fly,
I'd free my flock of dreams to swarm the sky,
Blind to both cage and fetter,
Blinded by sun and freedom of feather.

– Samir Georges

Voices

And Jesus gave us freedom
From our past sins,
So we took our souls to God
And asked him
How to keep a soul clean.
And in his silence we heard our answers,
And when we preached them to the rest
In his absence,
You heard our conviction.
And our faith was reaffirmed
In the hearing of our own words
And the silence of God.

Overcome

The final blow was struck;
the sun retired,
the moon began its darkling howl
across the mourning sky,
and all through the distant space
twinkled tears of grief.

As one heart, alone,
a victim to emotions
raging within,
it begs the world look
with every beat of its shell.
The heart begs the world look
at all the feelings it has held
the heart begs the world look at all the feelings
that it holds deep within
and struggles to contain,
the pain and joy
that rage to break free, to burst as one
but oh this heart holds them down
dams the flood, and with steady toil
it pumps and beats and threads the feelings out
in streams of red, and from a sea of yarn
it threads an ocean,
and alone it toils against the raging sea within,
till the sea bed runs dry
and the world lets out a sigh.

There is sadness in their eyes,
pity for the lone heart
that with a steady hand
wills a thousand beasts still.

Oh, the world has much pity for the dam,
for there is nothing like the rush of a flood,

the energy of a storm,
but to be left with this droll beating,
and the tameness of a steady hand
that maintains a crisp and boring garden.
But lo, the world does ask
that to what purpose build a dam
that will stand long past the waters have dried?
To what point stop a flood
that will in time flow and be gone?
To what end
bite your tongue and maintain a dream?
And with their pity the stars urge you
to feel all that you can feel.
Say all that must be said;
with pity they beg the heart explode
in a sea of red.

Instead the beat plays on,
for the stars do not know
what it is like to be a heart,
and the moon does not know
what it is like to own the sea,
and lo, who else knows
but we
what it is like to be human,
to dam the sea and make due with the ocean.

Pretty Angel

What's your name, pretty angel?
Do angels die?
Some say that not even time would dare to take you.
Then I'm not an angel.
What modesty, pretty angel; what is your name?
Do angels cry?
To waste your crystal tears is to dry the oceans and drown the lands.
Then I'm not an angel.
What is your name?
What is a name? Can you answer that?
Something I can cherish, something to be remembered with; what is your name?
You lie; it's a label, a way to keep me in a bottle.
If so, then no name is yours, because you were meant to fly before my eyes and leave me dazed, pretty angel.
Leave me alone.
Not till you ask my name.
What is your name?
You know.
I don't.
Of course you do; I am what you were waiting for.
Why did you come?
Angels do die, but time is not who claims them.
Who does?
Legends. You confuse me, I thought you were waiting.
No, I wasn't.
But you were expecting.
Accepting.
You accepted what angles cannot?
I did; I'm no angel.
I know, you're more.
Get it over with.
First, what's your name?
I forgot.
No, you didn't.

– *Samir Georges*

I hate you.
Why?
You left me.
I did, I can't be sorry; you let me go.
I let you go?
You pushed me away.
Why?
You wanted to be alone, free of fate, free of me, didn't you?
Can you take me home now?
One more thing.
What?
What's your name?
Unnoticed.
Pretty angel, I see you.

To Live, Flightless Birds

A single branch, clawed and pecked, fickle and straining;
Lonely nestling and father paw and peck at their home.
Lonely branch spasms in the wind;
Nestling and father paw and peck, yearn and whimper,
These flightless birds on a fickle branch.

Young nestling skitters to the branch's edge,
Peers over on to sightless depths,
Shivers, ruffles withered feathers,
Spreads tousled wings,
And loosens his fast aging down,
Stretches till overgrown talons graze the edge
Like endless days before, craning aching neck,
Eyes devouring the scene with a famished hunger—
And whimpers,
Turns to father and warbles in longing.
A sight that speaks of flight,
Dreams of swimming amidst the clouds,
To leave.
Slightest breeze carries words …
To live.

The father, neck cramped, tilted, eyes swivelling to and fro,
Cooing and cawing, talons pawing.
A slight breeze, decrepit feathers hauled away in swarms,
A forlorn sight that reeks of abandoned dreams.

Warbling, cooing and cawing, pleading and pawing,
Pecking in apprehension, neck swivelling to and fro in exasperation.
"To leave, Father! To stretch my wings,
Lift from them the smell of rot and loss.
To fly, Father."

"To fall! To fall, and to die!"

– *Samir Georges*

Wind whispers,
To fall, to soar, and to live.
Nestling shuffles to the edge,
Settles down amidst aching joints and a teetering ledge,
Peers down onto sightless depths;
They bellow to him
To fall, to fly, to die!
Fall and flutter amidst a shower of feathers,
Cramping wings crooked and futile,
To swirl into freedom carried by the stench of inevitability.
To fall, to fly, to die.
Little nestling whimpers; nothing so glorious about death,
nothing so glorious without flight …

Whimpers, shuffles forward, talons pricking oblivion,
Ruffles feathers, settles down,
Nestling wavers, branch bending.
Rotting down tickles his beak, claws dig deeper into branch,
Eyes feasting on sightless depths,
Endless fears.
They scream to him
To sit, to dream to fly …
To sit, to dream of revitalized wings
Stretching across the sky, an unuttered statement of freedom;
The shattering of chains every morning, with a stretch of wings,
The exercise of freedom
To sit and dream,
To live.

Empty Thoughts, Never Acknowledged Dreams

Empty thoughts, never acknowledged dreams,
they are not the means nor the end;
they are like wet tinder,
they do not spark,
and as you wait for them to dry and become something of use,
your life withers away and night turns to day;
you lose the need for fire.

– *Samir Georges*

Contemplating Quietly and Fluently Is He

Contemplating quietly and fluently is he
Not with speech but by mind and precision in every degree,
Congratulate those who assimilate to those around them with decree.
But he who cares not for the throng knows better than to be bound by such wrong,
For judgment is to be awarded by deeds best unknown to the judge,
Not as a tool to be handed down from a man to fool.

Once upon a Time Man Knew Only Shadow, but Shadow Did Not Know Man

Ignorance,
I wish you would afflict me till the end of time.
Ignorance, you're a petty thief that steals only what she wants,
For what you can't feel you deny,
What you can't see you will not seek.
Your epic simplicity draws me closer,
Yet reality holds me back;
Is it irony
That knowledge might cure you but can never substitute you?
We may live our lives in ignorance,
But who has truly lived their life in knowledge,
For no knowledge is complete.
Anything beyond these five senses that guide us cannot exist;
For you will it not,
This love that makes us lust,
This anger that makes us hate.

Feelings are jagged surfaces that grate on one another
And make of tinder fire;
Our mortality together causes a friction of contradiction.
Ignorant is he
Who knows not the sting of a bee,
Or the scent of a rose,
Or the prick of its thorns,
The kiss of a lover,
The sight of a hummingbird's hover—
Yet he desires not these things, for to his sorry soul they do not exist.

Can you imagine or begin to perceive
Not knowing death or suffering beyond the borders of your home?
Or knowing hatred and racism as nothing more than sounds?
Then again, that sweet soft touch of your lover,
That sense of accomplishment after you relinquish aid—
What is life without the borders of death?

– *Samir Georges*

A plain canvas is no painting to gaze at in awe,
And a painting without borders,
Oh it stretches on endlessly,
But it is depthless, as shallow as only paint on canvas can be.
But the detail of this globe we call Earth,
The knowledge that we thirst for,
The feelings we lust for—
All those jagged ends and scorching flares …

Ignorance,
I ask myself if you are worth the sacrifice.
It seems simplicity is a dead age,
And this world is worth much more than the other cheek.
Oh, my love,
As sweet as your kiss may be,
As alluring as your form may be,
I am a man easily charmed,
And though you may charm many and all,
Your realm is small,
Nothing built to withhold
The charms of the world without.

And so,
Ignorance, dear love,
We must part.

All Hail the Misguided Soldier, the Misguided Hive

All hail
The brave soldier
Who stands firm,
Like the fickle shell of a snail
Before the oncoming foot of titans.

All hail
The brave soldier,
A ferocious bee
Who strikes his stinger into the enemy,
Comforted by fleeting thoughts of heroism,
A safeguarded hive;
Thoughts that flit away in the wind
Like windswept pollen ambushed by desert
As the bee falls for the cause.

All hail
The brave invader
Who fells foe for his country.
All hail murderer,
Comforted by a noble cause,
Sent out on wings of glory to cut down fanged tigers,
Purging threats, safeguarding life,
    —the hive.
All hail
Misguided killer,
For all tigers are fanged,
All people threats,
All people life.

All hail
The weary soldier,
    sacrificial lamb,
Joined out of a desperate cause;

– *Samir Georges*

A squalling infant, a taunting belly.
And the weary soldier
Gives his sacrifice to the gods of the Hive
And prays for rain.

Many a Moment

I have many a moment,
moments by the handful,
and I walk down upturned fields
with my sack of moments in hand,
All my days, my nights,
pausing only for a moment,
shovelling seeds by handfuls,
shedding them like dandelion seeds;
and when that moment's passed,
I move on, pausing only to sow my seeds
in upturned soil, steeped in my moment's toil.

And if I could
but take pause
for a moment,
take a handful not coveted away
in my garden;
if I could take that handful
and gift it to you,
ah, it would be a handful to remember.
Moments between you and I,
not secrets in the soil.

– *Samir Georges*

In Repair

I find myself repeating
The question to your answer.

Why?
Why would you give me it?
Then take it away.
Why would you give me it?
Then tear it apart.
Why let me in, only to shut me out?
This feeling I crave,
This feeling I desire.
Your touch I answer to,
Your words make me whimper.
A small boy I am at your feet,
A small toy I am at your will.
Can I have it back?
Can I relish in its feel?
This feeling I pine for,
This feeling you give to me
When I am at your side,
This tingling in my heart,
That twinkle in your eyes.
May I have it once more?
These tears will not do;
This feeling of sinking I have
As my heart disappears.
Can I fix it?
Can my words make it better?
Can I see you smile?
Can I hear you laugh?
Can you make me fly again?
Can I have your breath upon my face as before?
Before that day when we died,
Can I please show you?
My shattered heart,

My broken words,
My cold breath.
Can I fix it? Can I repair it?
Can you fix it? Can I walk away?
I wish to walk away, but with hopes the phone will ring,
And once more your voice shall sooth my teetering mind.

Not for me, that is a dream.

– *Samir Georges*

To Die

Is it in me
to die?

Can I brave
the knowing life
of a man born who will die,
and he must walk the plank
with the spotlight in his eyes,
and can he stop
to ask himself,
am I ready to walk this through?
Can I face the light and die?

But oh what choice do they give!
What joke this is,
played on children—
walk to live, walk and die.

It must end, you see.
For some, it ends to start anew;
Others, it ends with grim fatality,
and oh so many reasons for why
it ends.

And I am supposed to be content
with your excuses?
I am supposed to be cowed
By mere words?
This bliss that is my life ends, fool,
and what words will mend my wounds?

It began, you know, with sweet breath,
or was it the impulse in my heart
to beat, make sound, and announce

"I am here,"
and the world knows that I am here
and let it do what it will with that knowledge,
It is I,
I,
that am here,
and always it will be, a life for me, a gift
given by whomever.
I am thankful, mortally so,
for the chance to be
here, now, whenever;
to be,
to blissfully be.

… and not to be.
Oh,
I give thanks with every breath
that I have become, and may for a moment more,
fight off the fate
of not to be.
Oh, these words cannot mend a wound;
no, fatal wounds do not mend,
but I am not a wounded man after all.
No, just a doomed man,
a comedy that wounds my soul, just not my body,
so that I may carry on, doomed to die.
But carry on, for what else can I ask for?
What more can you give
but the chance to be,
the chance to die
at least once?
These words are sympathy to me
and pity to you,
my friend, my foe,
because together we are doomed
and what poem is that
that I wonder, is it in you to die?

– *Samir Georges*

Whoever knows, what makes us ready—
but I beg you, dare me fear
the day that I must die,
or the moments of my life that throw my heart high;
dare me so that you can see
the resolve of the doomed
and the making of a man
from a child,
who may have once wondered,
"Is it in me to die?"
But now he has grown to face the light,
and doomed,
he answers the echo of questions past:
"I am doomed,
born to die, they tell me.
It scared me, you know,
but pray tell why should the doomed man fear
words that like saltwater fan my thirst,
when I am born to face the greatest daemon of all?
Pray, tell the dragon that breathes of air,
tell the dragon why into the sky it cannot soar,
tell the dragon why with every beat of wings it cannot live,
till the dragon to space succumbs,
to the world it yields
breath, and life, and the beat of wings.
Pray tell that dragon why, with every beat it takes, it cannot breathe
and roar and soar
all the way to the top of death, and glory in this sad fate,
cry tears of salt water and take joy."

Take joy in our breath,
the breath that is in us all:
it is in us to die,
because it is in us to breathe.

Beauty in My Palm

You are the wild flower in my palm,
With no stem to keep you anchored to this covetous earth.
You are the fragile thing I dare not cup,
As your petals whittle away under the wind
And flit unfettered in the air.

Exaggerated fear leaves my fingers numb,
Hungry need leaves my fingers twitching,
And my hand is paralyzed by turmoil
As every breath of wind takes another petal from me
And brings to my lungs, my chest, and my heart
An overwhelming scent of need.

You are the wild beauty in my palm,
And I dare not hold you to my chest,
For I fear to crush you,
To know firsthand
That caged beauty is beauty no more.

– *Samir Georges*

Dust Lands

Crusted eyelids rest idly
in a tomb of matching pairs.
A nation of dust and webs, stillness and decay …

A stir,

a tidal wave beneath the stillness.
Movement beneath the silence;
the eyelids shimmer,
and thunder strikes the chamber
in waves of flashes; eyelids break free,
shaking loose encrusted boulders
to tumble through the cobwebs
and settle in the dust.

With a great gush of desperation,
the sounds of thunder subside,
and now they are free,
a set of eyes amongst the many,
so grey, so weak, so frantic in their search,
filled with panic, eager to find
the darkness like before.

They cannot find it!
They scramble to hide, but lo, eyelids torn,
wondrous blindfolds, gone!
Averted eyes, the movement shakes the cavern,
causes an avalanche to cascade down,
showers them in an all too familiar grey,
unwelcome; they shake it off,
and now blazing red, they stare into the stillness.
So many new things—
dust everywhere,
webs fluttering down, recently disturbed.

The eyes lay still yet;
the world has darkened once more,
daring red eyes to turn grey
as the dust returns to settle,
and with their sight they are gone,
having seen enough of the world to fill
a lifetime of darkness
in but a moment's thrill.

And so those eyes remaining whisper;
in pairs of two they whimper.
The dust will protect them,
the dark so sweet,

and for those that cannot turn their eyes,
those that see the world fully
without the shade of lids,
there is silence evermore
in the resignation of sight.

– Samir Georges

There Exists a Variable

There exists a variable,
A variable that exists within the essence of subsistence,
Before a foreshadowed climax,
Beneath the storms of emotion,
The complexion of confession.
Even if the senses had retired,
And your chest's drum roll slowed down,
Your thoughts decompose in stillness,
Stiff and knowing.
Still, there is a sense that rages on in ignorance of the calm,
As the exhausted breath holds still
And as the pain deprives itself from indulging on the pained.
The winds, racers in the waiting, knees bent, eyes on the distance.
The behemoth of a bear, claw on the verge of ill will.
The mortal bent over, mid scramble, stilled under frozen doom.
Yet, within this tranquil scene,
    There is still a marauding feature:
The hand that immobilized time,
This severed limb that *(twitches)* struggles along mortality.
Now,
Let that claw come down, smouldering with rage.
(Still, that limb will twitch.)
For till it may ravage the flesh of its dread haunted victim—
And still it will twitch—
Let the pain indulge itself in the torrid sheets of an ill-advised affair
—And twitch.
This severed limb shall twitch, and each impulsive twitch shall echo louder.
Twitch!
Let emotion flare with passion and fury, revolt and obsession.
Struggling to twitch!
Let he on his knees speak with renewed vigour; let him wash his hands of guilt.
Try! Twitch!

Let your chest pound the drums of war till your blood dances to the rhythm.
FOR God's sake! Twitch!
Thoughts will lick to life in this furnace,
and with glutton devour the coal of life
Give it all! Twitch!
Your chest will heave up and down as the fire burns deeper into the caverns of will.
Keep trying … twitch!
Let those racers dash off at the sight of smoke and the sound of thunder!
Sooner or later … twitch.
And as the wheels of vitality spin just an inch above reality—
soon … twitch—
And the thoughts of those on board this one way journey shall scream out in unison,
"Let
there
be
hope!"
Twi … tch.

– *Samir Georges*

Words That Do Not Speak

Words that do not speak,
and in silence stare,
are words that are no good to me.

I beg them speak, tell me: feel!
Tell me write, and oh I would write.
I would write these words
to gift paper soul,
and for their company
these words I would gift with life,
where together we could feel
and talk the nights away—

if only they could speak
and gift me feel.

So Far

I travelled so far,
I had worked so hard;
Still the rain came down one dark night.
The storms attacked with no remorse,
Yet your tears carried the greatest pain.
Not even hails of needles could prick me bleed before that day.
I walked around this mummer's game,
Every footstep an echo of teardrops
As I swirled around, dazed,
And all I could see was your face,
Your smile,
Your life,
Followed by dreams of times
When rain was accepted with laughs and games,
When warm homes and welcoming beds were a place to rest.
Now warm homes and welcoming beds are a dream
that will not rest.

I built a shelter of wood and stone.
Before I arrived to claim it as my own,
The winds had harassed it,
And the rains had swept it;
The storms had ravaged it,
And the past had claimed it.
That shelter was my hope,
And past that horizon was you;
Now the horizon is clouded,
And you have vanished
As my hope,
As my tears,
As my cries,
As my dreams.

To rebuild that shelter, I must slave,
Till ever I must brave

– Samir Georges

Those hardships that have destroyed my hope,
That have shaken me.
Should I turn back,
After I have travelled so far, been driven so deep?
Your name is whispered as the winds blow by,
Your warmth is missing as the days go by.
If I said I loved you, would it be too strong?
Would you run away or turn your back?

Now I know what I have followed:
A dream, a vision, a hope, a rising sun.
But before I could claim it, the sun had dawned,
The birds had slept, and the moon had risen.

Barefoot and Bloodied

Barefoot and bloodied,
I run toward the blinding light
On paths of broken glass,
Shattered memories
That I can never seem to forget—
Barefoot and bloodied.

– *Samir Georges*

Check Mate

Ready to march,
The pawns would clear the way
For the cavalry marching on thunder,
Yet the opposition unflinching.

The monarchy would ponder,
Then they would build,
Not questioning their fortune
Over conquered land.
Yet beyond that jaded horizon, the sun would not stir;
Their bishops would bless hallowed ground
As their army would march,
And once at the end,
After claiming all that lay ahead,
They finally take pause
To look back upon the desolate treasure they have claimed,
This utopia they have formed.
Decorated by blood,
Sitting there with nothing but the sun and its heat.
Looking upon each other,
One challenges his brother.

The Sounds of Summer for Me

In the dawn of man,
The song of sparrows
Would tickle your ears.
The sound of summer
Was the hunt.
The sound of a spear whistling through the wisps of wind
Too fragile to see
But real enough to hear.
The thump of a landed meal,
The crackling of a fire,
The beat of bare hands on leather skin drums,
The sounds of purity.
It was the foraging,
The crunch of bare feet on virgin grass.
The sound of summer was the laughter of children,
Exposed in soul as in flesh, naked in dress,
Frolicking in a nest of wonder,
Imaginations soaring like young eagles unfettered.

Summer now:
It is electronic,
The beat of drums a modified bass,
The thrill of the hunt packaged tightly in an envelope,
Filled with papers of prowess.
The sounds of rippling change
And booted feet
Stampeding across well-clipped grass
In a rush of barely contained joy,
To delve into comfort and fettered flight
And attain the moments that yield us laughter.

Oh, the sounds of summer have changed,
But the joy they bring remains pure.

– *Samir Georges*

A Story of Loose Lips

Flesh on flesh,
Smeared art, rose-coloured lipstick,
A veil that lured him.
And in your moment of choosing, his triumph of weakness,
You ruined it so.

Your lips brush,
You tell your lie;
Your mask is gone, your innocents die.
Shaken, he steps back,
He sees your truth.
In shame he looks away,
Humbled, kept at bay.
You grin at him, clown face and all;
You slither the words, How the humbled fall.
He looks around, the dead at your feet,
Their blood spurting to the rhythm of a heart's beat.
His shield arm drops, the guardian failed,
Blindsided, the lustful hound wailed.

By the promise of your lips, your passionate pose,
His shield arm fell and never rose.
An ode to all the fools who lead us:
The mask of Lust will always bleed us.

Quizzical in Nature

First
There is the need of hope,
A desperation.
There is the belief of hope,
A manifestation.
Then
There is the understanding of hope,
A divination.
Then there is the writing of hope,
A salvation.
Then there is the preaching of hope,
A manipulation.
Then there is the deriving of hope,
A blasphemy.
Then there is the raping of hope,
A sinning nation.
Then there is the spreading of hope,
A commercialization.
Then there is the remembrance of hope,
A realization.
Then there is the questioning of hope,
An inquiry.
Then there is the discarding of hope,
A mistake.
Then comes the hopelessness of understanding,
An irony.
Then lies the realization of understanding,
A comedy.
Then comes the reintroduction of hope,
A mischievous cycle.
Then comes the substitution,
An analysis.
Here is the variable,
An assessment:
Hope is to religion as oppression is to slavery—
A simile.

– *Samir Georges*

Today, Not Tomorrow

I have been untrue
To myself and to my heart.
I waited for the questions to answer themselves,
I waited for the possible to become probable,
I cowered down behind shadows;
Even they shied away.
I cowered down behind lies;
Even they unravelled.
I cowered down behind those cowards;
Even they left in disgust.
Beneath the slime and muck of time,
I lie shivering in the cold.

Today I have said I, but never you.
Selfish is the soul that speaks
To itself as it leaks
Lies and deceit upon the shelves,
Shelves covered with hearts in jars.
These hearts that cry out the truth,
Their own echo is all they hear.
Today it rained crimson tears.
Beyond that cliff lies my bed.
I avoided the truth,
I avoided confrontation;
Today I opened a door
Only to shut another.
Time is a whore,
Time is the whore we all know,
The whore that stole it all,
Bottle up a heart in a jar.
She will reopen it someday,
As she has reopened secrets,
As she has stolen them back,
As she has taken my ego,
As she has taken my confidence.

Today I wait
As I have waited before.
A day passes as time laughs,
As shadows scurry,
As lies fall apart,
As cowards roar,
As time cleans out.
I shiver more;
My love to you is ebbing
A wait after another
I question my wait, how I rot in this seat
I question my wait as I hide behind deceit.

Thank you,
For on this day I know
I have wasted away before your gaze,
And your recognition is yet awaited.
Today I watch you get stolen away
And hope for time to repeat,
For if only a second before I could reach for you.
But now I wait
To wait again.

I am selfish,
I have watched,
I have gazed,
I have dreamt,
I have wondered,
I have left you there in that dark alley awaiting my arrival.
If only this seat had wheels
If only this dreamer had heart.
Now I wait for the moment I will rise,
And I wait
For the moment you shall beckon.
I shall cast my shadow upon the steps,
I shall shed my skin of lies,

– Samir Georges

I shall roar with vigour from within the cowering forms of many;
And time shall stare with awe.
Wings I shall grow,
And together we shall soar;
Through days and nights we shall dance
As time bleeds its envious blood.
Today I ask for you at my side;
Tomorrow I shall be there at yours.
This selfish capsule
Shall be a soul once more,
With all those forms casting shadows,
Soaring above the clouds of dreamers,
Paired off laying on the moon,
Howling for the world to hear.
Today, not tomorrow,
I shall be true.

Whispers in Silence

What keeps me awake
when the cool breeze bears whispers of things to come,
promises to be fulfilled on the morrow?

Is it my joyless moment of cognizance,
knowing that this stagnant night ripples from no real breeze,
only imagined promises birthed on the whims of a longing heart?

Yet what keeps me awake
is not these dreams of flattering winds,
but it is this night of lifeless branches and unrifled leaves,
the lack of real whispering winds taunting my heart.
What truly keeps me awake
is the silence of tomorrow.

– *Samir Georges*

Mechanical Man

My Mechanical Man,
Where have you been?
All alone was I in this desolate place,
But you left me knowing my need.
My Mechanical Man,
You come back now when it is over,
You ask me if I have learned.
My Mechanical Man,
How I've missed your steel,
Your jaded look,
Your emotionless face,
How you absorbed all my distress
Without leaving like all the others.
My Mechanical Man,
How I've missed your fake smile,
Your silent laugh,
Your gleaming stare,
How you shrug off everything
As though it is in your very stature to prevail.
My Mechanical Man,
You left when I fell;
Your unspoken words said it all:
Too many times have I fallen,
Your unmovable hand tired so,
But now you are back for more.
My Mechanical Man,
How deep you are,
Yet so shallow;
How you absorb so much
Yet reflect it back.
I learn today how it is and how it was,
How it should be and how you are;
Your love to me is undying,
Because nothing of existence can cease to exist.
My Mechanical Man,

Your cold steel by my side is all my warmth,
Your reflection of darkness is all my light,
Your expression of simplicity is all my depth,
Your lack of passion drives me forward,
Your emptiness completes me.
My Mechanical Man,
My Mechanical Soul.

– *Samir Georges*

Shrouded by Our Blessings

Shrouded by our blessings,
these feelings we share;
yet these feelings that differ—
flawed are our limitless minds,
clouded is our vision, hypocrisy,
heresy, and the sins of man.
Line us up and shoot us down; the future of our present.

A Good-bye

Wave,
Wave away the salt-ridden distress.
Your breath slides down the sinking pit within you,
A quicksand of hungering wants,
Fangs bared, coarse tongue whipping out.
No mother's breast,
Only your unclaimed breath.

A veil,
Mountainous,
Your lungs in your chest, near your heart, thump; you feel it.
A sea of pressure
Unrelenting, wave after wave battering this virgin shore.
White buds wilt,
Red heart shrivels, a raisin.
The shrinking shadow
Waves.

– *Samir Georges*

Paradise exists only where man has failed to.

Feather in My Hand, Ink in My Heart

Trickling over my mind
Came scampering the question,
This dilemma of a heart
Come running into my embrace.
Stricken with fright,
It asked me,
Father, why do we write?
I dipped my feather in the darkness of my mind
And brought forth my answer in kind.
I wrote of fear and the love that comes at a dreadful cost,
Of meaning and of the fight for knowledge never lost.
I wrote for voices unheard,
I cried for emotions long left unstirred.
The answer came to me as the tears wrote their own story,
Painted in pain was the imagine of a long-forgotten glory,
Emotions left uninspired.
Come to see what these words have conspired,
Come to see how these words have called them from their slumber,
To ensue in them an undaunted hunger.
Well, my dear son,
Here comes my answer to you:
I write not for you,
Nor for me.
I write for what is within you,
What has bubbled forth within me;
I write to stir the masses,
Unchained, unhindered.
Wilful subjects of our being,
They huddle in wait;
The towering limestone of their cave grow eon by eon
As they rot away, moment by moment.
I write for them.
We write for the grim,
The unnoticed prestige.
We write for what you have neglected to see,
To bring it forth before your eyes,

– Samir Georges

To fix your head with an iron collar,
To make you a slave of our direction.
We write to be your masters, when you need one most
We write to fix your gaze on what you have never lost
We write to drag forth from the depths of your inky heart
We are the harbingers of emotion,
Be it hate or lust,
The unseen veil of ignorance, or to shatter the blinding globe of pride.
We are the harbingers of sight,
With our binding collars, our guiding feathers,
dripping the black sweat of our laboured toil.
You will come to see
What has not been seen before.
We are
Fathers of a relationship sown by words,
sealed by the dawning of the sun, the dawning of realization.
We are
Your feathers, to your wings or to your ink,
And feathers will flutter,
Bearing you into the frigid embrace of the skies.
And when the winds will them no more,
We will descend upon the ground
And speak to the earth as we are reclaimed in its rough embrace;
We will write to the trees
when we cannot write to the birds, the sun, and the sky.
And through the trees we will see the starts,
And to them we will write about the shade—
Harbingers, indeed.

Peace Resides before the Fire and Once More within the Ash

I can't help but feel desire,
I can't help but conspire.
As my objective finds despair,
I yearn to retire;
As my mind churns
And my heart pounds in calling,
I find doubt within my existence,
I find failure where I have succeeded,
I find the future reflects the past,
And I walk in place
As I glance back.
I find my future falls into past,
Till guidance I seek,
Till mirrors I find,
Till wisdom I seek,
Till questions I find.
Answers form questions I seek to answer,
Until the pieces fall in place
As centers begin to spark,
As positions are replaced,
Questions seek answers and answers seek me;
Within my heart I find what I long for,
Within my core I find what I strive for.
This peace that settles within me
Against the challenges of a thoughtful life—
The mind of fire is at peace, when all it knows is heat,
So the mind of man can rest in knowing life,
For peace resides within the fire
That burns.

– *Samir Georges*

Till Time and Time Again

Every day I wake, I know I'm still asleep.
Every time I sleep, I know I will wake
From this dream,
This dream of finding you
Someday—
When everything we see outshines the sunrise,
Everything we touch is where it belongs;
When everything we taste satisfies,
And everything we dream hears our plea.
And we sit upon this rock, in this valley of snow,
Where the sun rises and the fruits grow.

I look at you and I smile
Till it's time to part,
And my heart cries out against what is to become
Of this world that has come to spoil me.
My soul rejects this body of mine
That rests on the power of a single soul,
And this love is no longer within.

Someday
I will find this haven;
I will find,
Find myself beside contentment
And my place in this world,
Knowing that the time will come
When they will find us,
When things fall out of place,
When clouds begin to take our notice.
Our hearts are dissatisfied,
But this rock will stay;
We will sit and watch
Until our hearts unravel like twine and thread.
Our souls lean upon one another and mourn;

Our minds resting in gloom,
Our bodies still in wonder.
Life was never our own.
We will carry our rock and find another haven,
And wait till time finds its way to us.
But as long as this rock will remain
A place for companions,
A place to share moments dreamt in silence,
This rock will wait for others as well;
It will watch them come and go
It will watch time take and throw,
For after all,
Havens in our dreams
Are the secret of dreamers.

– *Samir Georges*

Set to Bloom

Crippled,
A blanket spread across this lonely land.
Comfort for this desolate snowdrift,
But when peace is disrupted,
The blanket shifted.
There is the soothing kiss of time,
The scar brushed into the past,
And the fog would lazily settle.
This detested sloth of nature—
A spineless giant,
A slave of gravity,
With overgrown wings of cobweb feathers
To hide the scars of past.

But when nearby leaves would rustle,
A signal for the winds to roar,
To assault away this web of time,
To force those wings to flutter.
Raise this fog away from the beckoning earth
To soar into the skies
And nestle amongst the clouds;
Thus the winds would fade,
And looking down,
This universal giver
That shows sunlight to her children,
Satisfied beyond metric measure,
Gleaming with flaming pride,
Beaming before the specters,
Sending a showering presence of warmth
To complete the scene with a touch.
The flowers set to bloom,
Accomplished.

Roots Will Grow, Roots Will Spread, Let This Wisdom Be What We Shed

Deep within the scent of autumn, breathe in this ancient smell of growth.
Let the sounds of life fill your ears as all the horrors of the world escape you.
Let wanderers gaze at my ancient offspring, these trees of never-ending roots.
Notice the wisdom of their bark; an immense prosperity defies the sun.
Pluck my harvest and taste the secrecy of my importance;
I am a place that angels revere,
For I am here before all, and I will last of all fall.

– *Samir Georges*

Risk My Presence

Abused as a leisure of man
Till all is lost
And blood has ran.

Believe in me, for I am there
Within the roar of a lion
Or the growl of a bear.

Welcome me at your own risk,
For I have bred peril,
And I have raised aid,
But a disgrace of me man has made.

The Singer of Songs

Through the sands, this wolf would wander;
Along his journey many he would greet
With his howl of ancient splendour,
A tune of time and patience.
For him the sands would part in reverence, the ground quake in recognition.
From beneath this gap an earthen behemoth emerges
And erupts in fury as it glares at the boiling sun.
This feral rage of nature as protective as the warm embrace of a mother;
Giving way, the sun showers the wolf with its splendorous setting;
Then this bard will tuck away his timeless howl and venture to greet another audience.

– *Samir Georges*

Bounce

It lay in a room:
A raw heart of red,
Blue veins pulsing,
Ripples of red gushing forth in rivulets.
It beats, it pumps, and it bounces in place,
And every time it bounces it splashes in red,
And the whitewashed walls are ruined—
This heart is you.

There are four walls around you,
Three white with a splatter of red, and one red with no hint of white,
With a red pool of blood waving out toward them,
All around you as you gush and bounce.
And they look at you with hunger,
For you see, these walls have faces,
Four walls and four faces,
And they are closing in.

The face of the floor as you fell for the first time,
This face of remembrance, your first love and first regret—
It crawls on no legs, it slithers on no tail.
Opposite the wall of your future, the wall with no face,
The wall with only whiteness and the splatter of red,
And those two walls, the wall of your past with broken wings,
The wall of your future with soaring ones—
They face each other off, each racing to reach you first.

And then there are the two other walls.
On one side the wall of death,
Its face dark and simple, lost wings and a splash of red.
But as the three race for that warm little heart,
The last wall, the red wall, runs away, crawls and slithers, and life recedes you.
You gush and you pump.

As the three walls come at you, the waves of your life lap over their sides,
And the waves are pushed away,
flowing toward that last and far-away wall.
And as much as you bounce,
Waves of red and red walls shall never caress,
And walls of stone shall not be kept at bay by painted waters,
And life shall escape you.
All the while you bounce,
So bounce in red.
After all,
Red is a wonderful colour.

– *Samir Georges*

The Ravager of Redemption

Ravage and pillage the village did he,
This savage was a horror for all to see.
Born with power and a height to tower,
To grow and prosper into a meaningful monster,
Now he comes the age to begin another page;
His rule of tyranny will be ended with good intent,
A vision in his dreams, a vision of a dream,
A dream of peace and might within his sight, no blood or ruin to be seen.
This savage who could only ravage awakes to greet his servants as equals,
Yet in his absence the vacuum remains,
and
towers
grow tall.

Right There

More than you,
Less than me,
Who's on top?

Pet the pup,
Throw his bone;
Let them shine the shoes that equal them.
Below you,
Above me,
Spare a crumb,
Got a shoe?
Need some spit?

But He,
Nowhere near
You nor I.
The hand that lifts,
The shoulders that carry—
That is he,
The unnoticed prestige.
Let us take a bow
To bask in his modesty.

– *Samir Georges*

Ode to the Damned

A cold breeze sweeps through my bones;
Shackles take hold my flesh,
Subduing my humanity.
Wounds bursts forth in tears, outraged by the insults,
Protesting the steel around my wrists, ankles.

Exposed,
Snow prickles my naked skin,
Melting into my flesh.
Cold needles pierce into imperfections, exposed.
Sand slithers across my form,
Leaving scorched trails of blisters and pain.
Eyes pried open, the sun pounding at them in waves.
Noise pours into my ears, lies seep through the carnage.
My sand slashes at me, my sand rips me apart.
Snow I once welcomed seeps through me,
Grips my heart,
Grips my sides, pincers within.
As I feel everything from within churn,
Ethereal hands rake at the hope within me.
I try to scream,
My mouth spread open by braces;
Hands reach down to pull me up.
Salvation.
They reach for my mouth,
Free my voice.
They reach in
And muffle my throat.
My being protests,
My body wills itself cease,
To implode.
The hands from within hold it out
While the hands from without push in.

Rain pours down above me,

Rain of pity, of sorrow; the helpless sky speaks out,
The helpless sky protests.
The frozen winds batter the tears away;
My gaping mouth is victim to the selfish downpour.

Here on my sand, my snow, under my sun, I am
Prisoner
To everything and all.
I am without justice, without reason,
I am the object of rape.
To the birds in the skies, I am many forms.
The crying birds,
Whose frozen pity is damnation anew,
Damnation
For he who is prisoner,
tortured by helplessness.

– *Samir Georges*

Being

You are what you are; you aren't what you want to be or fear to become. You are the child of consequence, your being is arbitrary, you will be what circumstances will you to be; if those circumstances allow you to achieve your wants, then so be it. Always, with the passage of time, your being will come to pass.

Wonder Why

Father, why do people die?
Many reasons.
Like what?
Ask the killer, and if he has no form, it was natural.
Father, why do people kill?
Many reasons.
Like what?
My son, many things can be used to answer many questions.
Like what?
Me.

– Samir Georges

Cry Me a River

Tired,
Exhausted,
Spent.
So many versions,
So many thoughts;
Wipe them out, clear the way,
Ease the pain, end the fray.
Shame.
Turning to knowledge,
We seek the answers,
Sow order into chaos;
We acknowledge both worlds.
So easy it is to open,
Near impossible it is to close.
There is no step backward in growth.
Shame.
How I long for the memories,
Memories of restful sleep,
A departed conscience,
To swap mentality with an innocent.
It's a shame
We assume so much
Yet know so little.

Pulse

Contract,
Send my heart the impulse,
Command my life to beat on:
Thump thump thump,
Drone drone drone.
A slave of electrical impulse,
Biological study,
But at their loss, thump thump thump.
The replacement is as efficient;
Your presence is as commanding.

– *Samir Georges*

Ruins Reclaimed

Struck back,
The child cowers
As her tears wash away the scab of innocence,
And in her place grows another to tower—
Pillars of glory, symbols of might,
Ignorant to their birth,
Born upon spite.
And here mingle beings,
And here I watch these haunts
From mighty to small
In a maze of ruins,
That stranger I
Happened upon.

There glares a king,
Wrathful in nature;
Stutter does his slave,
Humble when broken.
There nurses a child
And scrambles a thief
As judgment is wrought.
Gods do beckon
To throngs for tribute,
Faithful and blind,
Eager to contribute.
Peaceful is the earth
Where seraphs mourn,
Devils are born.
Dazzling stars
Shine down upon them,
Sinister beacons
To strangers leer.
The sky rains down
Death and terror
As spectral life meets fate

And flesh meets steel.
Bodies meet ground,
Souls meet saviour.
Then,
Watches does the stranger.
Hopeful are they
As he wanders by
And reach for him,
But as their end is sealed,
Again hope is gone.
These spectral thoughts,
Ethereal, ghosts of memory no longer remembered,
Vanish into the background
As the sand washes over them in dusty tears.
These pillars of stone,
Children that once were,
I turn around,
Leaving these remembered ruins behind,
And reenter my world,
A world less real.

– *Samir Georges*

From End to End

One may lose himself,
From end to end.

Some men fight for freedom,
Others flee the strife,
But all those eternal scars are forgotten
In a single glance,
Where one wilfully succumbs
Within an aura lost in its way,
Meant not for eyes so easily ensorcelled.

One captive would paint
With new inspired zeal
A wingless angel,
Afloat in a pool of intentions.
Tears shed into a domain of solace,
Raw beckoning power draws the artist in
As he is wasted away before his creation;
Few break free, to lock away this addiction.

And the king takes up a new servant,

Keeping his new possession close,
As close as his greed, a lap for each,
Till a day long awaited.
Her wings would ruffle, and to the skies flutter,
And witnesses in mourning
Turn on their king.

When such fire can inspire such folly,
We may only pity these fools
And dream of the day an angel may grace our laps.

Blink It Away?

How do you say good-bye
When there is so much to acknowledge,
So much to leave behind?
These words, these thoughts,
Shocked back to life
To bear witness to—
No,
To be thrust into
This barren icecap of a once flourishing haven.
So little time was given;
Such a demanding goal,
To pour all the sand out
Before this hourglass finds the leakage,
Before all else disappears.
Faults first,
Then spill your heart
And finish it with hugs and kisses.
So routine.
Rather,
Take your feelings,
Strip them down,
Cram them into a canon
To blow their minds away.

– *Samir Georges*

Experience

Until we are able to scrutinize our emotions with the artist's eye, experience tells us nothing more than how emotions can cloud our judgment.

The Illusion

Distance:
It craves,
The distance craves to draw close.
It seeps into your chest,
Vines rope around your heart.
Your lungs, they clamp down upon them,
Tug at your chest,
Grip you surely.
You plummet.

– *Samir Georges*

The Illusion, Part Two

Flutter,
Your desires
Through every exhale;
Like vapour they depart,
surround you, envelop you.
You look beyond your throne,
Covered in the skins you carved,
Your fallen foe,
Your gaze lingering on what you crave.
Another breath,
It is yours.
Another breath.
You blink;
No breath.
You panic,
You look back;
Your servants gone, your throne crumbles.
The skins, they grow,
They howl their glee.
You blink;
No breath.
You plummet.

Three Ticks on the Clock

Let us begin in praise,
Praise of a situation.
This … comic fate,
To know your fortune, both foreboding and beckoning,
Yet have no control,
Only the knowledge, the destiny
To waltz.
For there is a tendency,
A circular tragedy,
To dismiss the truth until the lies are in place.
Time is death, and so death becomes time, for death will not come without time in hand,
And our death comes at every moment,
And once more at the end of our time.
And so where both begin and both end is the same,
For death is the end of our time, and life is its beginning;
They are the first shot in the air and the cross of the finish line.
And life and death cease to exist; we neither live nor die.
Statues first created and honoured, but forgotten, endure.
We do not live, we endure,
And time will end for all things, because all things must end,
Like the tulip
Wilting under the harmless winds of winter,
A winter that rallies strength nearest the end of the hourglass.

But there is a reality to time,
There is a method,
A sceptre of magical powers within our grasp.
Loot, brought back from the birth of man, ancient and holy in strength:
The power to postpone, the power to hasten,
The power to control the speed, the acceleration,
The power of vertigo and resistance,
Will power and the thoughts of man.
Yet the same way that hastens the hourglass' end

May also postpone the way to unravelling.
A man falling toward the welcoming earth
Flaps his hands as hard as he can;
Comic and foolish, the birds would mock,
But that man saw light for three more ticks on the clock.
Miners born into a life of labour, gold struck and riches bestowed!
… Green and sneering, the lone miner takes to himself;
Beneath the disapproving veil of night, he lulls away the gold,
And with a prize in each hand he is hunted down,
Trading a long life to be but a butterfly
amidst the petals.
Sorrowful drizzle soothes the wanting miners,
And down into the mines they dig,
Lulling back the few riches they conjured forth from the darkness
So that till the end of their enduring days they may believe
They own
And are not owned.
But the heart of a clock is wire and cog, and time is master here,
And for those who chose to live well,
Yearning to maintain their shining mountain,
Time ticks—a menacing cycle is at hand, a lonesome plan in play.
Here are slaves, given a choice they must obey: to wreck the mountain
In search of happiness, a gambler's sin,
Or to caress the mountain in search of respite,
A lover's downfall.
But as always, without a doubt,
There remain shores of sand, feast for the timely surfs.

The sun rises,
So to its call the scene awakes:
The child runs out of the cave, joy glittering in her eyes, light blazing about her worn face, innocence hoarded in sight.
Her aged features jade her joy, wariness befriending.
Follow her do fellow actors,
Falling into role as they are bathed in spotlight.
The father, light tumbling over cracked features.
The mother, too knowing of the world for the sun to play on her.

She basks in shadows,
Where her wisdom is in presence before sight.
As this superficial scene plays on,
Child growing in the grass, proud statues gleam down,
Unforgotten and renewed, the maintenance of pride.
A city promising to tower over them one day,
Bathed in shapely shadows.
No gold have they, no butterfly wings to fly above;
No ruins have they, no broken spires and broken ways.
But
As the sun sets on all kingdoms, unravel do the rays;
The petals tumble to the ground, and the earth quakes asunder;
The child grows, withers, and tumbles amidst falling flora.
Spires, both dull and majestic, tumble,
One with the rubble around.

And when the sun journeys once more toward the horizon,
Reaching out its splendid fingers to caress its lover,
They stretch far, they stretch thin,
Fingertips brushing the horizon.
As it stretches up toward the blazing globe, a chasm in the sky,
Fingertips graze cheeks and then withdraw,
Pulled aback by a grip iron strong,
The faith and love of stars and skies
Sent crumbling down upon fallen spires
As rays of luminescence untwine.
And the great globe of fiery passion unravels,
And the hand of time strikes thunder down upon that glass globe,
Shattering it into darkness.
The horizon shudders in pain
And fragments beneath the wrath of inevitability,
And tumble do the spires.

A peasant
Fit to scrub plates, relishing in the shadows.
And this lowly peasant,
Scarred of face, looks around aghast;

His simple mind ponders,
Did he scrub too hard? What role was his in the ending of things?
Simple-minded and inferior,
The peasant shrugs, shrugs off his incomprehension.
Why would things cease?
Why would great structures, built of brick and sweat of brow,
Crumble without force?
Why would the sun shudder and sunder without siege!
But the peasant knows not and shrugs, picks up a piece of rubble.
Eyes it.
Eyes another,
And wonders.
If he can work hard, sweat well, could he build …?
A kitchen, another pipe, another dish, to scrub till the end of his days,
To regain his place in this forlorn world.
Work, did this peasant. Wash, did this peasant. Scrub, did this peasant.
And die, would this peasant, over a plate and sweaty waters beneath,
Had he been peasant longer.
But no, this man was a worker, a builder!
Built himself a kitchen, he could build himself a spire.
So this man set to work,
And before his final days, he had built himself an empire,
And a people to go with, forged from his own body and soul;
He built them as he had scrubbed before.
But this man was no fool, he was no peasant or owner of serfs.
This man would rebuild his spires, he would rebuild his people,
For the day will come when they all must tumble and crumble.
But with his help, with his sweat and work,
That day would be far to come,
And his glass-built globe that shone light for all
Would be scrubbed clean till it glimmered as hope for his eyes,
The hope that one day his people would not crumble and tumble.
And let time throw fits of rage; he would throw his own,
And his children will live long; his sun will glow proudly,
His horizon will bear fruits unending! Till one day,
His over stretched and twisted hourglass, drenched in builder's sweat,
Must,
Must

run out.

It's Not Healthy

The way that child,
The way his gaze wanders,
Straining his neck left, ever more right.
Years on years he strains it,
And I can't help but think
That it's not healthy.

I've watched him long,
A creeping shadow,
an addict to pity,
And oh how I gorge
On his confused stare,
Like a deer thrown from a plane,
And the simple thoughts that race,
Like those I have seen on this child's face.
Time and time again
As he searches lost,
Lost in the dark,
And thinking
He should have a light
Where a deer should have wings.
Where is his light?

So I watch this little boy
Grow to be a young man,
Always a step younger than me.
I watch him grow
And watch him wander.

And he is now grown,
And he looks for that light
That he has seen
So few times in life.
And although not as scared,
Not as happy all the time,

– *Samir Georges*

His emotions curbed,
I still pity him,
For the light never stays long,
And when it is gone
We are always there,
Alone again.

Mountains

Eruption,
This haunting, terrorizing emotion,
This cord,
This ethereal torment.
Claws scraping,
Twisted biceps lurch my vessel forward;
Tattered feet scraping jaded earth,
An emotional grapple,
Refusing this crawling shell,
This once-dormant child,
Pulling forth on a taught life line
Till one day,
The scraping pain rose in protestation—
Too short was the cord,
Too mad must be the keeper holding the other end.
And rose did this merciless oppressor,
A rocky assault upon my person,
This mountain of fortitude, firm stone resolve.
No:
This uneven surface whispers through my shredded fingertips.
No.
Jagged scars paint rocks in tears,
But this smouldering volcano
Hears not the terror in the voices around;
It hears only the vibration of the cord,
Waves of craze;
It hears through them a cry yearning for longing
Through the mountain.
And to the lush beyond,
A haven, obsession.
Anchored is the cord
In a maiden,
Sleeping lazily under the shade of the mountain,
Caressed by my tormented breath,
Heavenly winds.

– *Samir Georges*

This cord that urges at this volcano,
This mountain that denies burning will,
This rocky cage that guards salvation;
The things craved the most
Torment the most,
Live to struggle against mountains, for maidens or for fame,
Fortune, desire
For completion.

I'm Writing a Letter to You

I'm writing this letter to you,
scratching with reluctance
words that shake a hand and mute a heart.

I'm writing a letter to you
with a shaky hand; I'm writing hello
and all those pretty things
that with time come and go.

In my scribbled script,
I whisper past the pleasantries:
with these words I try to understand
what makes those eyes wells
what makes the water so deep,
what makes the ripples that weep.

In my head
I've been writing a letter to you,
and it has come out long and littered;
like all good things, words were squandered,
what was said was wasted
by a yearning hand
that shook too much and could not draw a heart.

– *Samir Georges*

We Dreamers

We dream,
Dream,
Dream.
Dream of delusion,
Dream of what is not,
What we wish to have.
But
Dream we will,
Till the day comes,
Passes
Without a
Hush,
Quiet …
Whisper.
The day will pass us,
And we dream
Because we are dreamers.
Dreams are not real, dreams are fiction—
Then where rests the dreamer?

We are our own,
Cursed to dream,
Conjure up what we may never have,
Because
We dreamers
Fear what we do not imagine.
We fear what we do not consider,
What has not played over in our heads.
We fear that what we imagined, what we partook in,
Will be different.
We have dreamt up our fear
Because we who are afraid
Can only dream of being brave,
And we who dream of being brave
Do so out of fear.

This twisted cycle
Must
By all means
Stop.
Dreams are endless;
Our lives are not.

– *Samir Georges*

It Is What It Is

It is truly a sad day
When one gives up on his world
As a member,
An observer,
And a victim of its turbulence.
Many would judge,
Others follow,
Some rebel
All so hollow.

It is with no regret
That one cleans the muck,
Gives up on the fight
To settle with distinct recognition.
Live satisfied, leave a mark here or there;
Be able to enjoy the few ripe fruits in this soured field.
It is within realization,
We may note,
Each path taken,
Each choice made
With many effects,
Is one's own to decide.
But whether to follow, lead, stop, or fly away,
The choice is ours to make but for turbulence to direct.
It is with great resolve, we will abuse our lives;
It is with great satisfaction, I wash my hands.

It's Raining outside Today

It's raining outside today;
Can't you tell?

Even though the curtains are drawn tight,
And the only sound in this silence
Is the echo of my throbbing chest,
I know
That it's raining outside today.
And I know it
By the gloom in my heart.

– *Samir Georges*

Odin

Old God of man,
Rust ridden, cobweb stricken.
Crumble into, shatter into,
Stale, old, and brittle,
Lethal combination of decay.
Like all of man's ideals,
Our morals, man, will.

Stargazer, Hatchnet, Fangtooth

Fish sticks,
Little acts of indiscrete gluttony.
Mankind is special,
Given a globe of elemental genius.
Moulded,
An uncivil pile of clay
Intended for the king's plate,
Made into a steel girdle,
Creaking and cracking to hold his girth.

– *Samir Georges*

Lady

I came upon a regal maiden
Draped in a pinkish hew of light.
She sat nestled in a bed of auburn hair,
Checkered and entwined with lilacs.
Her supple form, raised up on slender elbows,
Held in the strong embrace of light, chin held up by pleading rays,
Exposing her supple neck, a heart-aching call to nuzzle.

My first fancy was to step in afore the light and hold her close,
But upon approach,
I feared the razor-sharp thorns that nestled her,
The vipers and the shadows that encircled her.

So I crept up to this bed of thorns and vipers,
And she looked down upon me with a knowing gaze.
I unrolled my heavy tongue and said to her,
"Name me a name, so that I can remember you."
Then she smiled the smile of a wizened parent
And sang unto my aching form,
"I have had many a name,
From the passion of the moment between star-crossed couples,
To the pride of a warrior on his country's soil;
From the cradling arms of mothers
And the wilful bond of brothers,
To that yearning that tugs on your heart, and tugs down at my smile."

And I knew her for Lady Love,
So I embraced the thorns and wrestled the vipers.

Of Man

Crest,
Pinnacle,
Wings displaying full splendour.
Sigh of relief,
The weight removed.
Lasso,
Net the mare.
The veil removed;
Realization, comprehension
Harnessed on, like saddlebags.
Crack of the whip—
The plummet of wingless flight,
The rugged thump and tumble,
The drizzle of rain,
The harsh pity of defeat.
Racking sobs, the weight of a burden,
The haunting demons,
Serrated maws come a callin'.
He scrambles, despair;
The rise, the steady plea.
Hands spread, the tears of sweat
Upon the horizon.
The rise, the fall.

– *Samir Georges*

But I Smell You, Somewhere Out There

There is a rustling of leaves
Somewhere out there,
But I cannot hear it.

Brown and yellow leaves, soft and sodden with dew
And decay,
And they smell rich, a blend of honeyed
Life
And fragrant
Death.

And these leaves, they do rustle
Somewhere,
But I am deaf to it.

And the breeze comes to me,
Bearing the promise of the sound.
I take in this rich scent, and through my expanding lungs
It settles under my skin, this rich scent of honey and fragrance.
It swirls over my heart, with millions of little scented claws.
It grabs onto every inch of flesh in my body,
and little claws drive me in search of the source.

For the rustling leaves—
Somewhere.

I roam this plain,
Lost,
And I am deaf to Life.
Blind to Death.
But I can still smell the rustling of the leaves
Somewhere.

I know you are out there,
A mound of sodden leaves, brown and rich,

Waiting for me to throw my arms into you
And bury my face in your warmth,
Your richness,
Breathe in this scent of life till it flows in my veins.

I know you are out there
Waiting for me to stumble onto you,
Trip over you,
Fall into you,
Soft and wet and rotten,
And be buried by the scent of Death.

There is a rustling of leaves,
And I wander
Deaf, blind.

But I smell you,
Somewhere out there.

– *Samir Georges*

The Sword, the Shield, and the Heart

I praise you
Home of Ahiram, your ancient king.
You, who grows cedars in her backyard;
You, who raised millions of children.
Whether they did you harm
Or left you blind,
Your door was always open, and your yard was always green.

Loubnan, you are not my country,
You are not a landscape of cedars and mountains.
You,
You are a patch of soil—
That same patch,
The one beneath my face when I fell,
When the taste of blood trickled on my tongue,
But always a drop escaped, landed on your rugged face,
Your tested and scarred face.
And when I sweat, of toil and pain,
When I run from your invaders,
My sweat trickles into my lips,
And I taste the pain I endure.
Always
A drop escapes,
And on your cheek it lands,
That rugged surface of root-ridden soil.
But you do not wipe your cheek of my blood and sweat;
Instead, with it
You built us mountains,
Crystal white beacons of your fortitude;
With it
You grew us cedars,
Vivid green emblems of your prosperity.
And when your foe would bring his fist and thunder,
Crush your mountains and burn your trees,
Always—whether we ran,

Left you alone and blind,
Or stood—made you hopeful and proud.
Always of our sweat and blood,
You made us roses,
Roses to place on our dead,
The dead we burry under the shade of your cedars
Under the protection of your mountains.

My Loubnan,
My patch of soil,
You are still not my country.
No,
Because my country is not a patch of soil,
Not without someone to work it,
A farmer to work your land.
Not without your people to stand proud with you.
My country
Is nothing without her children,
Without her fruit,
Without her cedars and mountains,
Her running rivers, the tears she sheds at our turmoil.
But whether fists come crashing down on us,
Or thunder shatters our hopes,
We will always work the land that raised us,
We will always be one country,
One nation
Of mountains and cedars,
Of hope and pride.
We will always be
Loubnan.

– *Samir Georges*

Blind Men

A child passes by
So full of joy,
Life,
A friend by his side.
Broad smiles smothered over their faces, veiling childhood ignorance;
Together they play, tumbling in the gardens of youth.
But before long,
before every scent in this blooming garden is savoured,
A thunder storm,
Shocking reality,
Unveiling their ignorance, exposing their innocence,
Shattering their smiles.
Great earthquakes, and the ground beneath their feet shatters,
And the duo is swallowed by a rising mist.
It enshrouds them, drowning away their cries,
Hiding away their tears,
And with that sundering, friends of old are replaced.
Shadows in the mist ever changing,
Sharp blades of green are dulled under the weight of dew,
All spoiled by the mist riding atop the back of time.

Slowly, like the growth of wisdom, the mist withdraws.
With every inch,
That once promising garden is returned to the sun,
And with every inch, realization
Where once there gleamed blades of green and welcoming rest,
Now sprouted weeds, thorns battling amongst themselves;
They sacrifice the shrubs and bushes of sweet-tasting berries.
And from within the unrolling mist
Strides a man in a suit.

With every stride he takes, away yield the weeds,
Crumbling under his very air.
And from within the foot tracks of his boots
Sprouts a structure breeding advances, great wonders to awe the world.

And what few roses remained in this scarred haven
Are sacrificed, to make way for more boot marks,
Wonders to awe the weeds.
Now comes another out of the retreating fog;
On his face is a contorted image:
A frown.
He drudges along a weed-ridden path,
Tripping and tumbling over scattered boot marks,
Each sprouting small, growing structures,
Orphan offspring of unthinking parents.
His tattered clothes, assaulted by the thorny undergrowth,
Hang on him like the shedding skin of a snake,
But this old coat would not leave its master.

Both men wandered on,
Blind to what was around them, what had changed
Till one day they walked toward one another
And by some random act of choice, or the strict lines of fate
Both blind men came full circle,
And without a glance, they strode past one another
As if the faces of their past were lost,
Altogether taken in the mist.

— *Samir Georges*

The Gleaming Crow, a Treasure before Her Eyes

Her flirtatious wings dripping shadows behind her,
Lush curtains, heavy, draped against the wind,
Bloated with darkness.
Her coiled claws, held to her chest, scraped one another,
The grind of nail on stone.
She cawed to him,
"I love you, I love you."
His fragmented eyes looked back,
glue dripping from their edges.

He said to her—
This wounded falcon,
The lasso tight around his yielding neck,
His once free main weighted down with black grease—
He said to her,
"I loved what you've taken, what you cannot replace."

She looked at him; he saw himself in her gaze, the falcon.
He saw himself in the black murk about his feat:
Its shimmers cried betrayal.
He saw himself,
His shrivelled form, his broken eyes.
"You will learn to love me more."

He looked at her; she looked at him.
She saw herself in the waters of her toil,
She saw her beauty, the beauty he must see.
He looked at her, her inky talons plotting their mischief.
"I am not yours to claim; you took me, I am no more."

"I will rebuild your world
With my hand."
Claw.
He stood above the jaded waters,

He remembered the rubble of his old home, the walls he had built.
She had torn them down and claimed him, his wings clipped.
She loved him when he flew;
He was no more.
Later she would know what he had lost,
She would lose what he cannot
Her need
They always do
All of them.

– *Samir Georges*

Genie

One night a genie came to me
And of reality he set me free.

Day

I Rose from bed this morning
and fell into another day.

– *Samir Georges*

Chasing, Racing

The child ran;
Monsters chasing, always racing.

The man is running,
    Crying and running,
And behind him came chasing
Abandoned dreams,
Nightmares of regret.
    Monsters chasing.

My Beautiful Cage

I look up on a crisp, clear morning,
And I sight the heavens.
I envision the gods of ancient Rome,
And I see,
I see the limitless world,
Ripe for my winged conquest.

But now,
I look up again, at a dark, dreary dusk.
A blanket of rippled grey clouds cages my vision,
And as the flaming red giant settles for the night,
It casts a deep red hue across the bloated belly of the clouds.
And I feel drowned,
A fish with no gills gazing at the surface of its cage,
Red ripples of cloud rolling over an enshrouding blanket.

And as my wings of naivety wither,
as I drown—
I gaze up at my cage wistfully
and cannot help but think how beautiful a sight it truly makes.

– *Samir Georges*

Tomorrow Is Another Day

The world grew bright, as it always did:

Squinting, the crippled boy rose on his arms, as he always did,
And upon his little shoulders rested a worn wooden plank.
And this plank, atop his little frame, shook and shook his arms as well,
For on this plank danced a troupe of merry little friends
To the tune of naivety.
And as his little friends did dance
This crippled world shook on weary arms,
Its little warped legs long ago wasted and spent.

And as the world grew dark and the music slowed,
The dancers, arm in arm, retired to warming beds, laughing;
So this little boy let out a little sigh,
Matched by the echo of their laughter,
And while all his friends heard was joy,
All his little ears heard was mocking.

And in this stale night, where no one could see,
The boy bent his elbows and fell there on the ground,
And he shook and he whimpered,
And he cried for a mother never known.
And when his arms stopped shaking, and his heart stopped racing,
His chest stopped sobbing,
He set his little face with a determined look as he gazed against the dark:
… Tomorrow is another day,
For the world to start anew, with old wounds anew.

The Green Checkered Face

I take firm grasp of the handle,
My goal reflected in the steel of the knife.
I put the knife to its green face,
Its checkered skin.

I flex my bicep, grimace with thirst;
I remember the day's troubles,
The day's triumphs. And I cut.
The blade breaks the rough surface,
Shatters the smooth oval,
And sinks deep into the soft redness beneath.
Juice flows over my hands, and I forget my thoughts;
I reach in and take firm grasp of the heart,
I wrench it out with red dripping fingers,
Slobbering it into my mouth.
The sweetness of the watermelon sends my heart racing with joy,
And I reminisce that I had forgotten the plate.

– Samir Georges

Goodnight, I Said, as I Tucked My Secrets to Bed

The world slumbers past the rise of the moon,
And the mist of dark creeps upon the world,
Crawling from the farthest horizon.

As the world falls under the mist,
The mortal genies crawl out of the cracks in the earth,
And one by one they eavesdrop on our dreams,
One by one they hoard our secrets,
Star-crossed lovers and dusk-veiled bandits.
And as dawn wills itself to rise,
The mortal genies take their well-kept secrets
And scurry into their cracks in the earth,
Ready to rise in the morning amongst the rest of men.

As the mist of dark fades away and recedes to the horizon,
And the moon stretches back to its eternal bed,
The sun greets it with a knowing smile,
And the moon replies of mortal men:
"Alas, if only keeping secrets from us
Were as easy as keeping their secrets from one another."

Pitter Patter

The grey boy wrinkles in the hands of greater things, wrinkles up like paper. Hands on knees and knees on chin, the wrinkled boy trembles in the hand of his mind. The room is dark, there is no light, and all he sees are shades of grey—his body of grey, the curtains grey, the wooden door dripping grey. And then he notices the red water beneath him, And it makes him shiver. He hears them outside. He hears the pitter patter, the barefoot running, the echoing laughter, and the feel of a cold breeze rushing down a hall. They remind him of his past, running down the hall to his father's room. And when the pitter patter of feet stops he knows the child has fallen, the laughter is the father, the breeze is the swinging of the child in the air, the whimper is his own in this dark, grey room; He lifts his knees higher. Uncomfortable as the red pool grows around him, he knows it shouldn't grow; he wonders why, whimpers in the dark, and wonders why.

The cold creeps up and he shivers, his teeth chattering away at the night and his knees knocking heads in comfort; The pitter patter of feet comes closer; the wrinkled boy sways to the ground. A grey feather stained in red. Wracking sobs pump grey into his once rosy cheeks. The pitter patter turns to thunder; it rumbles down the hall, rumbles to his room.

It rumbles and he shivers, and the growing pool of red ripples. He sees his distorted reflection in red: "Why am I grey?" He shivers again, he whimpers, tired of shivering and the cold and the grey, and wanting the red to go away. And yet he waits, shivers and dreads, and the thunder grows louder yet. His gaze fixes on the door as the thunder comes churning through. His eyes shut down, his knees lock up, and he trembles in the moment.

But as he yields, opens his eyes, the grey world melts away to the thunder of light, and he forgets all colours dark or red. All he sees is a little boy in his father's arms, and he remembers the car and the road, the sirens and the screams, and he smiles, thinking of the laughing and racing of the pitter patter, and wonders why he was so afraid.

– Samir Georges

The Sands Stand Tall

The tall rock stood on the beach,
Lonely amidst a multitude of lesser brothers.
He looked down on them, each a weak shade of brown,
Not golden like the sun that bakes them,
Not crystal like the waves that rake them.

The lesser brothers of the sands looked up to the mighty rock,
And they asked it, a voice as one
Yelling to reach its grand ears,
Yelling against the churning assault of the waves at their shore:
"Why so lonely, dearest brother?"
And the rock would shudder against the song of the waves,
The grand rock would yell down,
"How can I not be alone, when all my brothers have succumbed
To the beating of the waves
And became lesser men?"
And his lesser brothers turned away from his scornful gaze,
His brothers of the sand turned as one and faced the coming waves,
And they fell by the millions.

And the lonely rock looked at his fallen brothers—
How they still stood tall against the foe that felled greater men.
And in the light of this moon,
The tall rock stood small amongst grander men.

Loyalties

The king turned to the man to his left,
To his right,
And he asked:
Are you my men?
And they answered:
Not until you take your golden sceptre to our heads;
Will we take our copper sceptres to our loyalties.
And so they rode,
Fickle against the diamond sceptre of reality.

– *Samir Georges*

Oh Sweet, Sweet Dew

A bed of grass is so mundane;
It sways in the winds as the most fickle of things
And yields to the foot of man and beast and bug.
It is mowed and sowed as often as the grass does grow,
And as I stretch upon this brittle mattress,
I am dazzled by the floating skies, the whistling breeze,
And my comforting memories—
But not this dreary bed of grass.

And so love, to me, is like the sweet dew of the morning green.
As I lay back upon this nestling bed of grass,
It wraps my weary spine in a cool, welcome embrace,
And I think not of the dull blue sky, the incessant breeze,
Or my nagging memories.
Instead I think how the dampness seeps into my back,
And how the coolness spreads shivers to my every ache,
And I breathe a sigh of relief—
All because of this sweet dew on the morning green.

The Lying Man and the Clock

Let me tell you the story of the man who warred with time.
Let me tell you of the lying man who thought himself free
Of fate's monotonous rhyme.

This lying man would not a true story tell
To the masses: tales of himself in a regal crown, he would sell.
And they would ask: How come you're here, great king?
And he would weave tales of abandoning his office for a woman's ring.
Some would jeer, others cheer.
But always he would smile ear to ear,
At time in all grandeur he would leer.
To priests he would lament of his heinous crimes,
To never repeat them he swore,
Begging their pity and revelling in the new skin he wore.

So why, you may ask, does the liar lie of heinous acts,
When he could lie of owning the grandest tracts?
And the snake of snakes would slither its tongue
And shed its skin, a coat in its closet so neatly hung.
It would tell you a million tales, not one of them true,
And never itself shed in any hue.
For the flesh beneath may be soft and fickle,
But the skin above is always rough and brittle.
The flesh beneath, once shed, would still the beating of his heart;
The skin above, once shed, would instil in life immortality, a true art.
And always the happiest man alive he would be
Living the lives of any man his mind could see.

And so the lying man would not a true story tell;
The lying man would lie till the day he fell.
That day the king of kings dies,
The day the criminal meets his demise,
While the lying man that was lives on in every story.
As friends and foe would debate the king's glory,
All the while the lying man that is sinks deeper into his grave,

– *Samir Georges*

And that priest would remember a criminal who only mercy did he crave.

And that closet of skins would weaken and tumble,
The skins within gone brittle, discarded and humble;
As the lying man that was flesh and vulnerability decays,
All those skins he left behind, time will one day erase.

And so, lying man, you had smiled in the face of time,
Done no great deed but to steal what was theirs and mine.
You had fallen thinking you had bested the clock,
When only you had deafened yourself to the echo of tick tock.
Lived not what you were,
But what you longed to wear.

We Are All of Us Crazy

We are all of us crazy,
Mad in passions like a mystic forest
Where flowers swat away at bees,
And trees refuse to grow past crippled bushes
With fields of roses painting themselves black,
And streams beaching misplaced whales.
All the while fish seek to prance along deer,
All mad in this mystic forest,
Where fish can breathe aground,
And a rose need not fumble with a brush
In a forest now harmonious in discourse.

And so we are all of us crazy.

From those of us in a sordid love affair with gravity,
Plummeting fatal depths on bungee cords;

To those who live life like mutes,
    Afraid to share
Yet spill their hearts on paper, privy to the world;

While others they laugh at tragedy
And see black where there is white.

And all of us are afraid of words,
Handled swords that we chose to grasp by the point.

And are we crazy to act out of place
In a forest that thrives on ill-fitting puzzles.
Is it sane for the fish that has lungs to live beneath the waves?

Is it crazy to be yourself
And not an imposter?

– Samir Georges

And Always …

sometimes the snow falls in sheets of white,
a blanket of excited kisses, playful,
fleeting,
dampening your thoughts,
racing your heart.

and sometimes, the snow
falling in sheets of white
brings waves of brittle stings, sharp reminders,
memories in the ice that bite,
sinking your heart, making it cower.

you shiver,
your lips quiver, but it's not the cold,
not the journey through the snow.
it's hunching your shoulders,
bowing your head low,
lifting a weighted foot,
bringing it crashing down.

the snow bites at your lips,
dapples your cheeks with tears,
making you close your eyes,
bow your head to your chest,
and slave through sinking steps.

and always,
the last wave comes and falls.
and around your knees, like a rugged embrace
lies yesterday's shower,
and as the sun rises,
that soft pit of tingling kisses and prickling bites,
it wavers under the needs of a new day.

and this caked ground quavers and sunders,
flows away, leaving you damp and shivering once again,
so you lift unfettered foot, send it forth onto cleared paths

and march into the warmth of a new day;
and the dampness on your clothes is no match,
the dampness in your bones just a scratch.

but for the dampness in your chest,
the sinking of your heart …
as head holds high and shoulders lift,
chest is pumped to the heats caress—
so comes the healing of the sun, to mend the damage of your plight.

– *Samir Georges*

Fear

A blind man stood at the edge of a cliff …
and in his heart he knew no fear.

I Love You Because …

I love you because…
You make this quest,
This mission to muddle fruitless words together.
This question that riddles my soul
Meaningless.

– Samir Georges

Desert Paths

It's a long march across this fated desert;
No paved path across shifting dunes,
Only shaky legs to pull us across the distance,
No flat hoofs to rid us of these sinking steps …

We feel alien to this path, fated to its hidden tracks.
This crooked trail that shrivels giants.
Nourishes clinging shadows.
No serpentine glide across scorching sands,
Only blistered feet and a shambling gait.

It's no wonder we fumble with the weight of the sun upon bent backs,
On dune-laden paths through shifting days,
Lost on an endless leash,
Pulled in by consuming mirages,
Tethered by bouts of misplaced hope.

We flounder through the endless sand,
Drown under waves of heat, relentless,
Sinking deeper into this crooked path
On crooked legs.

Oceans Deep

I can't see the allure of romance,
all those words, like bridges avoiding water.
but when I see you,
with beauty like poetry written about your skin
so shallow, like only words and bridges can be,

I trace the hand that wrote them,
find this poem both ends and begins
with two rivers, eyes deep with water.
and like no other rivers can be, these are oceans deep,
the waters dark and unrevealing in the shadow of bridges,
where far below there are no words or echoes,
only silence,
and far below
there is a world of water I do not want to bridge,
a world within your eyes
that begs me explore.

oh, there is no romance in my heart,
but there is adventure, in the very beating of my life
there is adventure, and I see the allure
of a surface that with my touch ripples,
trickles down your skin
and writes with words bold and brazen
about the hidden beauty of a strange and distant world.

so I have no words
for romance
when I am but a simple explorer,
gazing into your eyes in silent askance
of a visit, to sit beneath these bridges built,
and brush my hands across a heart oceans deep
to bring myself closer
and burn these bridges down.

– Samir Georges

Writer's Block

Birthed in the womb of my thoughts,
A bird of stone carvings, written secrets and envied flight.
Heavy stone sinks through my head;
Chained hands surge forth, grasping,
Links snap taught, fingers brush your elusive wings.
Yet you escape and plummet.
Roving eyes swivel upward to see you soaring down;
Lidless, ever glaring, they lock onto your secret carvings.
But too fast you shoot past their gluttonous prying
And down through a troubled canal;
You battle against the sighing breaths that send you upward,
A wordless plight for expression.
But rock wings beat through the oppressive heaves,
Unexpressed, to fall down into the pit of my stomach
And forever disturb my waking muses,
Another block of words unwritten.

A Wise Life, Understanding Death

One day I chanced to walk by the spirit of a dead man,
And he looked unto me with wizened eyes,
Asking: "Child, what is life to you, this darkness and this light?"
Aloud I said:

We rise into the light when we are born,
And we fall into the dark when we die.

To that he shook his head and clucked his tongue
In fading, said to me:

"We are thrown into the light when we are birthed,
And we are pushed into the dark when we are killed."

So this lurking haunt left me wiser than my smooth, unwrinkled face would show.

– *Samir Georges*

Tension Waiting

The swordsman who draws his blade,
Heart racing at the keening of steel on scabbard,
Tension coiled, poised for the unleashing,
Held back by muscles tight with glee.

I am as the soldier, held in stance,
The lioness crouched beneath the concealing grass
As it sways back and forth, as insects sing along the day,
Her every breath is halted, her veins do not pulse,
And just as the swordsman stands
They are statues in this moment,
Statues of derision,
Mocking with their stillness the very charged tension within.

And I am as the lioness frozen before her pounce,
Coiled with motivation and purpose;
And I am as the tongue held with words clinging off its edge,
Ready to lash out and strike with direction.
But I am as the frozen purpose, held tight
Waiting for a warrior to stand before me,
For a reason to uncoil, to lash out with words and pounce.

But I am now as the pen halting before the purest of paper,
White and supple, in askance for the lightest touch.
A slash of the tip, drawing lines in ink,
Lines like a hunter's bowstring, taut with intent.

As the pen lies frozen above its prey,
The falcon petrified aloft still winds,
I am the need, coiled tight like a wound jack in the box.
But alas, there is no victim to frighten,
No prey to pounce upon, no sword or bared neck to slash against.
And I am here, with pen frozen, ink ready to be drawn taut,
And I have naught to draw in the ink, no prey or purpose to evoke.
I am coiled tight with energy, but it is release that so eludes me;

I am coiled tight with purpose, but it is direction that so denies me.

And here I am, pouncing at ground before me,
Slicing away at the air around me,
Scratching away with a dry pen, on paper still white in askance.
I write about …
I write about the coil within and the lack without.
And alone I wonder,
Is it enough, is it enough to go on, a wound-up box,
Waiting for the slightest touch, the weakest parry,
to live?

– *Samir Georges*

Dancing with the Shadows

Resting in restless waters,
The gentle waves lapping against my arms, my chest,
A fickle surface that at my touch melts away.

A wave of my arm and the ripples scatter,
Parted but not parting, ever clinging to my tingling skin.
And as the light plays across the shifting swells
Where around my limbs dance the wavering waters,
I float like father to this fragile scene …

And I know why it is I love the waters so much:
For it is here where I may be like the sun,
Like the sun and its light and the shadows thereof;
Here where I may shine my arms through resting waters
And like shadows they scurry from my path,
And like shadows from my attention they are born,
And I am a god, giving life to ripples and waves.

It is not the stillness,
Not the resting in caring waters
That is so dear to me,
For I am not the sun, not a god amongst the waves
If I do not shine and splay my being across its surface,
And as the waters cling to my limbs
And are parted but not parting,
I may play the game of gods
And dance with the shadows.

Cold Ice

Ice flower
so cold I cannot touch,
but need forces my exposed fingertips,
and I brush them against your crystal petals,
and bitten skin comes off willingly
to cling to your cold disregard.

Ice flower,
frozen as you are
against this hot desert wind,
seeking to slice your bitter air
to melt away droplets of beauty
from your seductive petals.
but oh, seduction and its lure:
my hot breath comes fervent and warm,
but I do not draw back into my lungs cool favour.
no, your crystal buds do not yield fresh melt water
to sate this parched throat.

no, my breath comes back short, sharp and shivering
as if the unforgiving hand of winter
had battered my very heart away,
and the cold wind gusts back into my lungs
and shrouds my heart
slows the pumping of heated blood
and leaves only a brittle casing
of cold ice.

– *Samir Georges*

Painting Alone

He is himself a painting,
Sitting there on a painter's stool upon the cliff edge
jutting out over a vista to the envy of gods,
where the skies reach down to touch, to but experience
this view to capture the soul.
Where one could but look into the distance
to drift across the world and savour its every pleasure
and forever be free
with but a look.

And he is himself a painting,
this man who sits with brush in hand, and like a shipwrecked sailor
parched and dying of thirst
sees before him ocean waters of crystal blue and honey dew,
and cups in his hands a depthless morsel,
raises it to yearning lips
to drink from the ocean—
just so, this man he lifts his brush,
and with every stroke
his parched tongue laps up the sweetest drops of honeyed milk
as indulgent brush laps along the canvas
and paint sinks deep into every pore.
This man, he drinks the ocean.

Yet he is himself the painting,
and when he is done, when his throat is sated,
he picks up yon coveted ocean
and tosses it over the picturesque cliff—
    down and down it tumbles …
to crack and shatter upon a mountain of like paintings.
And this man, who is he himself the painting,
is a man alone with his scenery,
a man alone, and he paints for no one,
and this picture, this lone man with none to savour his plight,
sends his brush and his soul over the vista
and drowns in the ocean

Lament of the Soul

Shall we
Lament about the soul,
The snap of the branch that you hold onto
When we snap it upon the drum that beats out life,
Withered and fickle.
And with the last reverberation of its breaking,
The echo dims and dilutes
Our sense of longing.

Oh, let us lament about the soul
And all it has come to mean,
An escape from drifting, that echo never fading.

Oh, anchor me,
Dear soul of mine,
Anchor me and never let me go,
For without you, why without you I would truly be lost;
And keep me alive some more to the beating of this drum.

And whence it snaps
In the drunken beating of my life,
And the echo booms no longer,
I beg you all to lament about my soul,
For it has gone
And now I am lost,
Drifting with no anchor, and I will find no purchase.

– *Samir Georges*

Opinion Worms through Me

Can I be of a matter to tell you something?
Can I tell you about my pain,
this writhing worm in my gut?
This parasite that so feeds off me
and drives me in return?
This parasite that I have grown to call a friend,
a companion in my solitude,
for if not for this parasite, who would share the knowledge of my pain?
No, I have nought but this parasite,
and now, alas, now maybe I have you as well.

Oh it started, my friends, with the need to voice thoughts,
to take stands
and give shape to being, to essence, to you and I.
Oh it started innocently, as with so many dreadful things,
and it started only to then grow, for such a thing cannot fall, cannot dwindle,
for it is an expression of being
and has but one foe:
one edge honed keen enough to shatter its illusion.
And oh is death the edge to shatter all things grand and small.

For to be, my friends, to be is to stand;
to be is to take shape, take form
like a lonesome drop of water alone in the vacuum of space,
assailed on all sides by a demanding hunger,
a hunger this lone drop, this poor champion of being
must sate.
And so to be is to take shape:
to gather about one's self beliefs and matters,
to be is to form a drop of water in the midst of draught
and fancy yourself a bane to the universe and its empty might.

Why, look now to the past,
to the greats of Alexander, that cascading waterfall,

and look, oh look how he shapes
this full pregnant wave giving birth to opinions
to stands and positions, to the grandest decisions,
to a being supreme.
And when came that waterfall to a sizzling sun,
in twain was each drop carved,
And this honed edge bit through intent
to fell so easily this cascade of opinions,
a grand champion if any ever were.

Ah, my friends, how I rail at this worm within me,
how I call out its lies, at the injustice of it all.
I rail and I wail and dread the coming of the sun,
and so dream to be an ocean,
to drown a sun not grand enough, to storm the universe forevermore.

And this gut, this pain that I share with you,
it taunts me, a coil within that will not rest
for that blade's edge hones itself still.
And I cannot help but take shape against this futility,
I cannot help but rail,
take a stand and define my being,
for in a vacuum I must stride,
this space I must seek to champion
as my heart thumps in dread
and my watery form shakes away in tears.

And I share with you, my friends,
the knowledge of this worm,
the coming of the blade
and the futility of it all.
Forced to take form, to form opinions and matters,
to be a self against the knowing
against that painful worm
that tells me with every churn
that the blade hones itself, and I cannot but go on,
go on to that dreadful day.

– Samir Georges

And till then I must gather about myself shields and arms,
thoughts and comments, ideas and engagements,
and believe, or dare to believe, that in rotting away I leave behind that ocean
that in facing the sun, this ocean can be passed on to others.
And I dare to live this deceit,
knowing that this ocean is my own,
and all I will leave behind will be the memory of its vapour,
and with me all this shape, this will to struggle on,
will fall to this fell worm.

And yet shape is forced upon me
to share with this fell company,
and I would have it no other way.

Dour Company

Oh, leave me be,
Leave me be,

I cry out in silence.

It is enough to bear the pain the world lashes upon my back,
Held upright but driven forward
By gifts, gifts to quell the curses.

But oh, leave me be,
When the lash is in mine own hand.
Oh, leave me be, you thoughts that pain
And you sharp pangs of regret.
Your dread company is no comfort to a weary heart,
To a shaking lip;
Your caress is no reason to still.

For you bring me no gifts,
You bring only curses,
And in my life,
In my life I have no want for curses.

So please,
Leave me be;
I cannot bear your fell company.

But oh, I am dour company indeed,
And still I cannot leave myself be.

– *Samir Georges*

Fighting the Good Fight

It's not about where you sit,
Upon a mound of golden silk,

And it's not about with whom you sit,
Amongst loves and past memories come to reminisce.

Being in joy, finding happiness so raw,
As to be felt in every atom, every flake of skin—
Not joy to send you soaring,
Not happiness as a seed that would sprout you wings,
But joy like the warming rays of sun
soothed by a gentle breath of wind,
And that joy is in your very bones.

Oh, it's not about where or when,
As I sit here across an empty chair
In just another café.
This joy that loosens the muscles of my neck,
It's about the words you say
Aloud or in silence,
The words that bring silk to life
And keep the hounds at bay.

Joy is my struggle, and I fight it with a smile,
For it's not the company or the coffers:

It's the words I say
While I sit across an empty chair,
And these words, they evoke my joy
From the very cadence of my marrow,
And in my eyes this chair does dance,
And this café and the world around strum along
To the ringing in every cell;
They dance along to the words I say against the silence,
In tune with the pulsing of my very bones.

In League with Others

I am in league with the roses,
Petals askew in a scarlet conspiracy.

Oh, I am in league with the roses,
Swaying along in this lover's intimacy.

I'm in league with the devils,
A mob together raging alight.

I'm in league with the devils,
Our very breaths fanning our damned plight.

And with the clouds I have marched abreast,
Bringing storm and heavens in tow,

For amongst the clouds I have marched abreast,
Purpose seeded in the sky to grow.

I am a hired sword in league with grander designs,
Through all of which I am never prone.

Yes, I am a hireling in league with foreign designs,
Happy that I am never still to stand alone.

– Samir Georges

I Miss the Dead …

I miss the softness in their voices
That I cannot recreate;
I miss the warmth of their silence
Where now only cold remains.

And I know, oh how I know
That they are long gone,
And I have been long removed
From those fuller times.
But still,
When I feel around my heart,
I find that it is missing things
Parts long lost and dearly missed,
And I sit here, feeling fatally incomplete,
And I know that I can never be whole again.

But I still miss the dead,
And I miss the times
When I never knew
That I would live on,
Missing the days I was whole …

    So I still miss the dead,
And the times when I was not hollowed by loss,
Living every day with a lighter heart,
So far from the times
    When I would never be whole again.

And now, so far removed
From fuller times,
These few missing holes
Let in a chill wind,
And somehow, these missing holes
Leave my heart heavy,

And I know that it will grow heavier yet,
But I dread
That when I am lost,
I die not just incomplete
But empty—
    Empty of all I could yet lose.

– Samir Georges

Holding Its Breath

My wrist curls upon itself, and my knuckles shut their eyes,
and my shocked fingers
hold onto this pen in an iron grip, sweating dread,
while upon the tip of this quivering pen,
the drop of ink that hangs on by its calloused fingertips
dares not look down.
For my heart,
    it now holds its breath—

and my world waits for it
    to let go.

Breath Let Go

The earth shudders, and the dust of a thousand years lifts
up into the sky like a blanket thrown aside in exultation,
and beneath this blanket, plates grind together
    in sudden need
A craving to bring dried and edged flesh
with the moisture of the oceans above
    together once more
and cry out in the joy of ecstasy to release their pressure
    And be at once reconciled.

And the world lets out its breath,
gives up what is most sacred to it
in reverence of this Moment:

And I dare say this moment is mine, yours,
to the child that toiled the fields,
hoe in hand, minding the patterns in the soil,
the patterns in the soul through which water poured
and escaped in pores like water through a parched man's fingers,
and patterns fled this farm,
leaving a parched man lamenting the presence of fingers
in times of thirst.

And to the child toiling
    in the fields,
the pattern is in the pitch of his shoulders
and the pounding of the sun,
the pattern that should never leak
through unseen holes.

But it seeps
down his back and across his fingers;
upon his hoe it dribbles down and finds the escape
of patterns long lost,
and the sweat of his toil

slips through the gaps in his soil,
and the heaving of his shoulders
is lost with the patterns.

So this old farmer, he does not tread his fields,
sheltered behind wood and warmth of fire;
he huddles in his world of four walls
and dares not the fields outside,
where await the failures
of his toil.
And when the earth shuddered
in joy of this moment,
knowing in its wisdom all that was to be known,
the earth shudders and the dust of not so many years,
it lifts into the sky like a cover torn away in exhilaration.

And beneath it all

Sees the farmer

The pattern of his toil.

And lo and behold,
it was not wasted,
but a hand's width beneath.
The soil that caked his world
and by his own hand,
hidden as it were,
the patterns of his toil
and the story that is told
bittersweet,
In the exultation of a breath
Let go.

Knees Bent, Untying the Knots of Fate's Cast

Back to the roots ever weaving,
Hands to elbows, sweat streaming.
Back to the roots whence the seed began,
Deluded to think that along the path you ran,
The roots had not snaked behind your every stride
And tangled your feet to fall hands first into your erstwhile guide.

Back to the roots where it all sprouted out,
And take grasp of the past and heave with a shout.
How your roots have brought you back matters no more,
For you have fallen back into knots that have tripped you before,
So take grasp of the roots and yield to your past,
Knees bent, untying the knots of fate's cast.

– *Samir Georges*

Letters Bespeak Words

I think that when my fingers brush
these keys,
I sense my poem forming
before it blossoms in my mind,
and it speaks of a relation
between my touch and each stroke,
the gently bending,
the wilful obedience
of each key press,
each typed letter that bespeaks
words.

and it is this story
that writes itself
with every brush,
and I know my poem
before it comes to life,
for the touch and the stroke
live on,
even when fingers are sheathed in pockets;
and my poem,
although not alive in my head,
has never died and needed rebirth,
for the poem is always there,
ready to be written
between each brush and stroke;
it is written
in the very electricity
binding my fingers to the keys.

Mining

The world moves on,
and so do you;
on gears we grind
like a mining crew.

– *Samir Georges*

Betwixt Bars

Can you feel?

Can you feel the tremor
That rocks your world,
That shakes the cage
Like a beast trapped outside?
A beast raging against the bars,
It lifts, it throws, it rages.
Can you feel it?

And in the aftermath,
You can hear the cooing, cajoling
Of puppeteers laying strings before your bars,
And they croon and cluck like fretting hens,
Petting your bars and calling for you
To reach out and take these strings,
Tie them where they cannot reach
Deep within, where no one else goes.
And let these good people in;
They preen, and you shake your head,
Seeing the gleam in their eyes.
Oh so like the beast's
Cooing, cajoling, cawing,
And oh, how you can feel it …

But I'm here, so hold on;
I'll sit by your bars,
I'll sit by the door
Right beneath that lock that turns from within.
And I won't rage, or set the siren's call upon you.
I'll sit by your bars and keep you company,
My friend.

But cold bars let through a breeze, friend …
Your sharp breath is not secreted away,

And with every breath you take,
Your lungs are profaned,
And you cannot hide
Behind bars.

You cannot hide.

From my voice, or my presence, or my eyes,
My eyes that see too clear,
And you cannot hide from what I see,
What you can feel
Pressing in from us all.
So just let us in,
My friend,
Let us in, for we will not be kept out.
Life does not surrender, life does not hold back,
Life seeps through
Every crack.
And be assured, there are cracks everywhere
Where there are breaths to be shared;
There are bars to let them through,
And you feel it, don't you?
That which you see deep in my eyes,
You feel it;
That feeling so clearly reflected
When I look into your soul,
That fear alive in my eyes
That rages on within you.

But don't fear a battle you have lost;
Do not fear the day you must face the world.
The world, friend, has never
Turned its face from you.
And the rest of us,
Well, we are not so brave,
We are not iron bars moulded to flesh.

– *Samir Georges*

That fear you see is real,
And it is ours all,
But we cannot hide
From what burns within.
And I will not die
Hiding from life,
And I will not cower when I tremble inside,
I will not rest in a cage when I am tired,
And I, friend,
I am so tired
Of living here on this floor
Between the bars you built around yourselves
With only inmates for company.

Ruined with Words

All those fine moments
Ruined with regrets,
Like sheets of crisp paper
Beleaguered with words.

– *Samir Georges*

My Doubts

So many greats,
Gods and wizards,
Weavers of word and song
ink and paint,
Weavers of tapestries and life.
And they are makers of greatest prose
Heaped with praise to shadow the world's gold.

And here I am,
Whittling away at this meagre branch,
Hoping,
Dreaming,
Straining
To make of a meagre branch,
The most awing stick.

Hiding

A small, tight crevasse,
A fracture in this mountain side,
A small slit of dirt and grime,
Sharp pains and unforgiving edges.

The Hider scratches and grunts his way in,
Deeper into the tight abode,
Gasping and groaning,
Skin tearing and splitting.
Stones rattle, and his little body writhes;
Shallow breaths.
His chest pushed tight on jabbing edges,
His back arched away from stretching daggers,
A gymnast in some sick event.
Stomach curled tight,
Eyelids shut in some mislead search for relief.

So he hides, deep in this unwelcoming refuge,
Hides from his fear, from the world outside this little pit,
A sordid existence of damning rocks
Giving only pain.
Short breaths
And shut eyes.

– *Samir Georges*

Shades of Pearl

I'm tired and worn inside,
All grown up,
And it's changed my eyes …

And it leads me to ask,
Where is the beauty of the pearl?
Is it in its murky depths
Of opaque whiteness?
The potent charm of a white canvas?
Where is the beauty in a pearl,
When I cannot see its heart?
Oh, but even then it calls to me,
And now that I have
Pearls for eyes,
Is there beauty
In seeing nothing
But desire
Reflected back to me,
Denied to me,
By the bluntness of a mirror?

So I have pearls for eyes,
But I remember
When they were diamonds.
Oh, there was desire then,
Much unfulfilled need—
But that was just another facet
Of my diamond eyes
And their many brilliant facets.

The light shone every which way—
Back then
When the light shone every which way,
And I saw so much more

Than mirrors and pearls;
Back when
I had diamonds for eyes.

But something changed,
As things are want to do,
And that something,
It turns diamonds to pearls
And dreams to regret.

Or was it …
Well, could it have been
That I committed the grand sin?
The betrayal of childhood:
That betrayal, when you regret to dream
That so morphed my eyes?
And proved too potent a lure
To so turn my diamonds to pearls—
That regret even themselves
In that sightless reflection
Of blank desire?

And even now I lament
That this poem was written
In shades of pearl.

– *Samir Georges*

A Struggle to Be

It's a struggle
When vibrations strangle strings
In calloused hands,
And it's a struggle
That sets that guitarist's tone.

And it's there in a smile,
When eyes trap flame and
Desires rattle a forceful cage,
And the struggle is in the smile.

And I struggle for every breath
Because the very air that I breathe
Is charged
Like thunder in heat;
Charged with the friction
Between a stagnant surface
And the roiling thunder beneath;
Charged with the need to meet the very clouds.
And the air,
Oh the air I breathe,
It carries the cries of lightning
From far, far away,
And that cry beckons
The clouds within,
And there is righteousness in its need
To strike at my heart
And make of listless clouds
Harbingers of thunder.

Make Your Move …

In recent poems
I have fought the same demon,
Wrestled him to the ground,
Stared into his face.
And he stared back
As feelings raged across the surface;
He hid nothing from me
Because the mirror has nothing to hide.
And I cried out against all I saw,
But I did not look away;
I held that stare,
I hold it still,
Even though I wish to look elsewhere
Onto a prettier scene.
That would not so ache my eyes
Or tire my soul.

But here I am,
Staring my demon in the face,
And he does not smile at me in a sinister way.
No … he but waits
For the next move,
Oh, for the next move
Has always been
Mine.

– *Samir Georges*

Pretend

I won't pretend
to know what to do.

Just take my hand
and lead this dance;

I won't pretend …
to know these steps.

But let's pretend
we know how it goes:

the chemistry of the dance
and the love in between.

Sweet pretending,
Step by step.

But let's pretend
I know these steps.

Shall we dance?

Anchored on the Shore

It seems
the longer I wait
on this dry shore,
the farther you get
as I watch you sail
away
from my place
on this dry shore.

the winds pick up,
and your sails unfurl,
and with every breath I lose,
watching you drift away,
a gust of wind
sends you with blessings
of breaths wasted
on the memory of an older me
that I had dreamt away.

and I see you still,
distant as you are,
going to that place.
I dreamt for you,
a place that grows farther still,
as I dream for you
grander things
and grander places
that you will visit.

And on currents
that seem to flow
to the beating in my chest,
you sail farther still,
and with every dream I breathe,
you sail farther yet,

– *Samir Georges*

and you're so far away now
from where I am
on this dry shore.

and I wonder if things would have been different
had I not dreamt you away
and kept you here
on this shore,
where I can still see you.
no matter how far you sail
from this shore,
that you have never left
that I have never left
but have dreamt of leaving.

The Lonely Dark

Night and day:

It's always tug and pull
Between night and day,
Between lovers never entwined.
Oh, it's the crave to caress
The longing stare that spans a chasm
As the sun fades beneath the dawn
And the light slowly retreats …
The night, edging into the world;
The first flirtation, so appetizing …
And it lunges forward,
Seeking to touch, grasp, hold!

But always too late,
Always the divide too grand.
Light draws away,
The darkness settles,
And it is omnipresent:
A depth of universe
So vast, so full of stars and worlds,
Enshrouding like a blanket of secrets and untold deeds,
Grand and great,
Mighty, unquestionable,
Inevitable
For the dark to encroach, encompass and overwhelm …

This night,
It stands all around us
With no peers and equals.
The light long gone, long faded,
And the night, it but waits.
Every night, it but waits
Till the dawning of the sun,
That first sign of light …

– *Samir Georges*

To fade away
Because the night waits
And fades alone …

Our Very Own Nights

I try to share
My precious little time
To ease the passing of the night
As I watch it fade.
Every sunrise
As I watch it pass.
And the night is grand,
Gracious and loving,
For it holds my hand
As I go to bed
And face the dark.

– *Samir Georges*

Bringing the Shuttle Back Home

Happiness
Is not the spawn of pleasure
And desire;
It's not the child
Of satisfying need …
Oh, happiness,
It's not a lot of things,
It's not the smile of the sated
Or the promise of more to come.

Happiness,
It's not a lot of things …
But oh,
so much more:

Happiness,
To me,
Why … it is a feeling on my face!
When the muscles on my forehead
Relax, and my brows float above my eyes,
And my eyes,
    They are set free:
To see;
And my cheeks
Are free to stretch or pout,
And my lips, they can curve up or down!
And I can see so much more
When that weight is lifted
Off my eyes.

And happiness
Is all that I set my floating sight upon,
And all that my roaming eyes behold
Is rendered weightless.

A Tough Question I Was Asked

And so, poet,
Riddle me this:
What do you want life
to look like?

I could never paint
Pretty pictures,
So I tried using words
To weave pretty paintings.
But alas, sometimes weaving with words
Leaves me tangled and confused,
And so I end up riddling to myself
The answer to each question …

But this is a time of seeking
Clarity, and the time to unravel
Some knots,
And in the spirit of this season,
I tell you that what I seek
Is comfort in special shapes:

A shape that lies by me
And in so doing fills the chasm
Between my heart
And succour.

I seek to shape
A comfort
Like sets of diamonds
Before my eyes
And so see a clearer world.

And I want to see
In my life

– *Samir Georges*

Comfort
Of every shape
Like that by my heart,
And before my eyes
Like that deep in my soul, my mind.

A comfort for all those I know in my head,
And so a comfort from all my aching thoughts
And restless nights,

A comfort in every breath:
And when the last breath escapes me,
I want it to be absent of doubt,
I want it to leave me with comfort in its deliverance,
And in so doing I will know
That I have died with comfort in each breath,
And so I live
To meet that end.

Appreciate the Song

Appreciate the song
that with tune
and beauty
of sound, like tangled
dancers,
singers entwined, arm and leg
with the song,
sings itself a lover
to dance with.

so appreciate the dancers
that dance upon the breath
of music,
the exhale of instruments
and the power of the life they breathe
that brings dancers to your ears
to spread into your mind,
ride your very lungs,
and dance on out
atop your every breath.

so appreciate
every breath made with music,
every dancing step it takes through you;
and the song bird:

appreciate the song bird
that sings to life your every breath
in the presence of a life
sung
with every breath.

– *Samir Georges*

Breathe into Me

Gently we sway,
glide on thin winds;
little dancers with gentle feet,
hoofed like doe, silent prancers,
winged softly, webs of feather.
we flutter up, flit around
like wisps of smoke;
we entwine,
and like frosty breaths
we escape
up above
the world so high,
flirting dancers that whisper to the sky,
you and me, we like wishful dancers
playing in fields of ghostly whiskers
cannot die.

No More than We Are

I gave you a broken rose
When I promised you a field,
Bouquets sprouting fresh about your feet,
And I promised you the forest painted by my own hand
Of greens and sights of colours to fill the world.

But I handed you a broken rose,
Red and green and snapped in between
On that empty field one day,
And could give you nothing more
Than myself
and the colours therein.

– Samir Georges

North Star

Let your fate take root
on hard rock, tangle and bury
before the coming storm.

And before the coming of the storm,
amidst a garden of your crafting
beliefs and memories planted,
and like seeds watered,
Take root amidst your cherished greens;
take hand in hand your memoir
and brace with rooted, tangled feet,
mangled,
The coming storm
come to wash away,
come to whisk away.

This is a magical storm,
something fantastical,
    like myth was born
from your hands, as you shake them left to right
and wrestle from them
    seeds.
Trample on your well-trodden soil,
and in waves bead your sweaty water,
shelter little sprouting
to take shelter in his shadow.

Did you nurture your garden
like I have nurtured mine?
    Mine, lush with little ideas,
lush with my graceful evasion
of duties unwatered
moments hoarded,
lush with little trees that in my shadow

do not grow,
and their little fruits, so sour born.
Yours, that garden, a gnarled tree,
posies tangled on mangled fields,
bounties of fruit in your mangroves,
    the many children of our labour,
all alike stand before the storm.

    Dark clouds gather,
broil forth like no afterthought,
an army summoned to war, the tax collector come for dues,
and bubbling forth.
Comes lightning and thunder like sickle and torch,
come to reap the song and sun.

And it is in this shadow they finally grow,
and gnarled hand takes my own.
    I will not rot away on my own;
I stand before my fated choices,
and together
our bonds new, old and gnarled
stand firm these moment's beliefs and
    creations.
Children and parent, arms locked, heads on shoulders both,
eyes cast out and tears exhumed
before the coming storm.

Our legs take root in our
garden soil,
and we cling to what
we know,
we hold to what knows
us—
but the storm is just
so vast,
and our roots are just
so shallow.

– *Samir Georges*

A King Rides

It is only conquerors who have lived,
only kings who have grappled the reigns
and lurched upright upon this wild steed,
ridden and been bucked, trampled and shucked
like peasants one and all, into the earthy mud;
but it is only riders who have lived ...

The world will throw you off at every turn and step;
the steed bucks and bites,
and many are we who walk alongside
with a healthy fear and clumsy resignation
to slough through the mud, behind a plowing horse,
trudging waste deep and squinting through the sludge
behind a stamping steed, as brown as the mud beneath.

It is the conquerors who unsheathe the blade,
raise sword to naked neck, make people bow their knees
and with sword gently suggesting
the master mounts,
the conqueror rides.

And lo, the world is made to buck,
and we hang on for dear life
as one way or another,
as earthquakes shake countries,
the world will buck and all must fall.
For the stallion rides, and we but walk,
and all that fall, can fall alive—
but it is those who conquer truly
the bucking steed and falling defeat
that die well before the fall,
atop the stallion's back
and feel not the mud,
for the conqueror rides,
refusing the mud;
the conqueror rides and refuses the world.

For the world was made to buck
and so cling on for dear life,
for the world will be free of you,
even in your death free of you,
but still ride, my friends,
and like kings conquer the mud
and ride.

– *Samir Georges*

She Came to Me, in Clandestine Robes

she came to me, in clandestine robes,
and we revelled in her secret.

My Eye for a Kingdom, My Other for a View

There are islands
that ruled a world,
islands like no islands ever were.
Trees to top mountains and beasts like giant titans;
islands like none ever were,
that ruled the world,
and from each island
a different world,
a different sight,
and a different kingdom
for each island
that ruled a world.

We speak with different eyes
on haggard cliff tops,
and against the pit beyond
echoes our argument across mountain peaks,
because we speak with different eyes,
and you stand in a forest of shrouding closure
and, with eyes transparently veiled deliver your calm riposte.
I scowl at your eyes that speak such lies
And, with eyes blinded by the sun behind mountain peaks,
glean that your soul
sees a disguise.

– *Samir Georges*

Turtle Man

Sing farewell,
turtle man.
Hum your tune
out loud
to this empty desert,
turtle man,
when your shell is caked and broken
and your shield is split in twain.

Sing farewell to your only friend,
your comfort from the heat,
when turtle man is standing naked,
baking in the sun;
he sings farewell,
and who is there to hear?

His only friend,
a place of solace
that all his life he wore,
and that place has broken down;
he sings his silent farewell
to the empty desert,
this little turtle man
who sings to no one
and sings out loud …

Who is there to hear
the farewell tune
sung only by turtles
alone in the desert,
where the snakes are burrowed deep,
safe and deaf
to the singing
of a lone turtle
who's broken his shell
And misses the echo of its singing.

The Watch on My Hand

Time holds my hand
as I struggle with the vision before me;
and the vision before me
is all I see of my life;
and what I see rages in scenes I can barely decipher,
struggling to make sense
of the bitter pang that stings my eyes
with every scene; and I blink often,
I blink often, and I miss yet more scenes,
and it waters my eyes, but the sting lands deeper.

I close my eyes and breathe deep,
wanting to lean on, my only trustee.
Oh tick tick, timeless as you are,
tick tick tock, the clock
that weighs down my arm,
your grip surprisingly light, considering …

But something about the gentleness of its weight, such a charm,
though I confess, I wish nothing more than to lean on that weight.
I wish that it manifests a wise sage,
someone I could lean on,
timeless, steady, not weathered with age.

Still, I must make due.
Just hold my hand, you jaded creature,
and with your fickle touch teach me something new;
teach me that everything is growth;
teach me that every time this vision is not sweet,
and its bitterness seeps through my senses,
and this feeling of weakness and regret
that inflicts me, as I watch my life, as I watch every life,
teaches me that with every prick and bruise,
every miss and glance,
I grow.

– *Samir Georges*

And your grip on my wrist tightens,
and I look at you damningly,
and I see you have not grown, your weight is the same,
a gentle pressure, no more.
But you tighten yet, when the stubble on my face grows,
and the pits beneath my eyes deepen
at the very sights I live.
Now I glance at you not with accusation
but beseechingly,
loosen, I beg with my eyes
that have seen a life flit past.
But even then you tighten more,
and there I stand hand in hand with my only friend,
learning that with every moment's regret
and with every look cast out,
I grow, and the hand tightens on my own
because my hand has grown so big,
but yours still so small
and as only the truest friend
You hold on still:
as the pressure mounts,
the feeling swells, I grow more,
and I know there comes the time when I will feel my hand no more,
and I would have grown all that I could grow;
but you'd hold my hand till then,
hold it through every moment that I live.
So you teach me, my friend,
that I am growing, and that every chance I miss and moment I fail
is not a wasted moment or a foul moment;
it is a moment I have spent holding hands with you,
and I cherish it, for tick tick comes the time
when we will hold hands no more,
and I know then I will miss you, friend.
Just forgive me if I look at you accusingly again,
saying with my eyes
that we should be embracing, that we should take these moments
and forsake the distance between us.

Yet would I be saying this, friend, had it not been for your gentle,
lightly weighted touch?
Would I so want to hold you, had you weighed me down since the start
Or held me close all this time?
Would I be so grown, so loving of you?

No. I will grow like this, with but your gentle touch,
and when it comes my time, and I feel your clasp no more,
I will know then
that what I wanted all along
was but your touch,
and to know you were there
with me all along,
this watch on my wrist
and the clock in my soul.

– *Samir Georges*

Seeds

the numbness spreads
over the seed planted in snow,
and I'm running out of time
as the numbness spreads
and settles with a firm grip
on my shoulders,
leans over
to read as I write.
and the numbness spreads
with whispers in my ears,
crystal clear sounds,
cars with tires rolling by:
as the numbness spreads to memories
old as my childhood self,
when cars would roll
on screeching tires and sputtering engines.

as my fingers slow,
I feel it spread—
the numbness is in my nose,
the back of my head,
the core of my heart,
and the distance from my soul.

And it still spreads,
hands all over me,
an unwelcome touch
stretching all over—
the seed I've planted in the snow.

Eyes Speak

It's hard to write to you
through all this paper …
it's hard to see your heart
from all the way here

so let's talk softly, you and I;
let me lean in cheek to cheek,
hear my whisper
whisking past your ear,
brushing your nape.

and now   you hear me.
we have been fools I think, you and I,
searching for the echo of a voice, lost in the dark,
and it comes muffled and broken.
it's a little funny, sometimes sad,
but I miss the days when voices came clear,
when I could hear your heart, honestly.
it's sad that all I had to do was whisper

so I whisper
in your ear, with your head resting here on my lap,
and what would you hear me say?

    I look down into your eyes,
and the moment starts
when all I do is fall,
just fall, and when I've fallen,
maybe you've flown
up into my eyes, and we can see each other then,
and only then
I can try,
try to give you all I can,

give you this moment,

– *Samir Georges*

a moment when I fall into your eyes
and invite you up,
up into mine,
and I can finally give you a moment
when you are known,
loved for all that is inside those eyes,
loved not because of words—
    words are wasted on paper.
loved because with a look, I know you,
and I give you this moment, when you are known
and truly not alone,
as I see past your eyes
to hear the words they whisper.

The Devil Walks

The devil walks
gets tired
and sits,
and while the devil sits,
the devil picks up a tired fruit
rotting, and with jagged nails he peels
slowly, the tender fruit bruising,
and he tastes it, smacking his dried lips,
and the devil eats
decayed fruit and sour wine—nothing lush and sating.
Then the devil rests
and resumes his walk,
and later the devil sits again,
rubs his feet
and goes to bed,
and in the morning
he breaks his fast on curses and lies—nothing so filling as figs and nuts—
and begin the devil's walk again.

His walk
on the road our thoughts paved,
where all that grows is bad and unwell,
to the cross our words built,
where flames dance and all is unwell;
and he is condemned
upon christening,
upon the hearing of his name,
and the wobbling of his first steps
to walk a road less travelled,
to be the leader
of our very own crusade,
armed with words
against himself
to see him burn.

– *Samir Georges*

Our crusade of one
and many,
on roads first paved upon his birth
to bring the devil down.

The devil walks,
the devil eats,
and, pelted by our stones,
he does but sleep,
for what we sow
the devil reaps.

And there is justice in punishment,
there is reward in reckoning,
there is bitterness in my mouth
as I say these words
and pity
    the devil
his due

Simple Fears

They tell me,
"keep it short and keep it sweet."
more and more I hear these words,
the allure of the simply spoken.
more and more a fear grows in me
that one day, this will be but a token.

— *Samir Georges*

Blue

Blue is the colour I see before me,
like waves chasing white ocean mist.

Blue is the colour
that hovers above me
and sneaks around me.

Blue is the colour of my sheets
that hold me snug at night
and ease me into cloudy skies.

Blue is the colour of my blood,
the hue of my sweat;
blue is pumping from my heart
in waves crashing upon the misty clouds above.

What Are These Nights

What are these days
but passing nights
in the poet's dream.

– Samir Georges

My Lady in the Sky

It's those tiny little stars.
set like jewels amidst her opaque shawl,
held tight about herself against the cold of the distant sun;
those little jewels that seem to glimmer only for me,
inviting me take off that sombre shawl.
But I dare not stretch my hand to but share a warming touch
and expose her bared shoulders to the frigid night.

Beneath the Sun

I will not kill this fly,
Because we are both together
In our wait for that final dawn.
And lo, how frightful that hovering hand must be
In the shade of certainty.

I withdraw my hand,
Admitting impotence
Before this fly
And shadowing sun.

– *Samir Georges*

Hanging Flags in Space

What is there to say
when words run out,
and this pencil hangs limp in my hand,
soul like a

suffocating man,
the absence of air.
Roots and clocks,
shiny things and flocks,
wisps of air waiting in a dank room.
The door opens,
outer space,

leaves a limp man.
So ask him to see the beauty
in us all;
ask him to see the fullness
of you all;
ask the paper to encompass the balloon.

Discomfort adieu,
there is no cure for the sickness
in mere words;
there is no cure for the sickness
that makes of words

lifelines
that hang limp
in outer space,
where the limp man sees

the world so far below.
Floats his paper hand over us all;
globe in hand,
moments pass,

gestures lose meaning.
He floats away;
a desperate yearning to his eyes
latches on that sphere,
blind to the paper flag that waves before him.
Waves like a wounded heart sinks to the depths,
and we can but watch; above a murky surface
the heart that sinks, waving as the ripples do,
the flag that flutters limp
with no soul to give threads steel,

the leaflet is caught in the wind.
Have you ever asked, does it struggle?
Does it clutch that fence with purpose?
Does it yearn to hold its ground?
Fighting every tug and pull with a twist and turn,
latching on to all objects protruding—
sharp cuts, tears, thrashing
up, up into space it is taken;
Do we hear its cries?
Do we know its pain, stolen, robbed, deprived, inhumane?

He still hangs there, you know,
limp in space; but the wind that that took him
held him tight all the way,
threw him, discarded.

He does a turn, a twirl,
flaps his wings and floats;
he's lost track
between a twirl and swirl,
where he was, how it was,
and he spins away.
Tears go unheard,
whisked away
by hapless winds
that bellowed within.
His turns lose speed;
the paper cannot encompass the balloon
with all that air inside;
his turns lose speed,
limp alone; the heart sinks.

– *Samir Georges*

Deserving

We are all deserving,
to be held
in sure arms, with surer grip
offering solace, and a place to belong.

You deserve to be hugged,
and in those moments of comfort
when you feel another's breathing so real,
and you breathe in answer to their offer,
birth a union of moments eager to be
and exhale, into a welcome embrace.

We are all deserving
to be held,
and in those moments,
eager to be held,
You deserve
to be understood.

Moments

Moments
live themselves

and for every moment more
expect to live
in a moment's notice.

– Samir Georges

Tiptoes

She tiptoes
About my nape,
Giggles, and my sight she escapes.
Scampers about my ears—
Never long enough
To catch her meaning.
And after she plays
Her games,
There is silence about my person;
She is gone
Like a whisper.

Busy Hands

I have busy hands,
busy building walls, diligently stacking.
These busy hands
build so high, they guard so well
walls that do not weep.
And there I am, swaying on top;
they shoo me off, beg me come down,
go inside
out of the rain, but I won't,
not today.
The rain like tears all around me
mocks the dryness inside, where you cannot cry—
all kept clean and neat
by busy hands
that piece me together
when I fall
from wall to floor, come tumbling down.
Oh fragile me,
I've broken again.

Mended and scolded by tired hands
and on crutches, they tell me
sway
no more
atop damp walls.
And fragile me agrees,
sits dry and sheltered
in the shade of lofty walls,
kept tall and standing by fragile hands,
shaking hands that keep
the prison doors.

– *Samir Georges*

Both Sword and Shield

This life is mine,
tis mine to wield
like weapons drawn,
both sword and shield.

Hunger

Nothing daunts me more
than these blank pages
before my hungering soul.

– *Samir Georges*

Written Thanks

I thank you
with every word I write,
every confession I pen.

I thank you
with tears of joy
shed in tears of jet black ink,
to the sound of rapping on gentle plastic
with every tap tap of the keys.

I thank you more,
for holding me
when I run for your embrace unbidden.
I thank you so much
when I run from home,
escape that place
that begs escape,
and rush first and only to you.
So thank you
for reading my words
and embracing me,
when the embrace I feel at home
is a pressure that I cannot take.

I know to you I can run
And, with all the thanks in my heart,
embrace you once more.

Closing Curtains

Hover above the stage,
departed from mortal ways, everydays,
departed from its long life partner, its home, its shelter,
its shell a discarded prop …
It floats away beyond sight, fades into our daily lives, into our past,
and away from this final chapter,
soaring as angels would dream to
into an endless sea of childhood memories,
beneath a drowning sensation it can only embrace.
But time rushes along
and, with the force of wind that speeds along,
casts it out of the reminiscent past …

To float the cosmos, to promise the sun and lay with the moon,
but nearing the edge of fantasy, awareness,
nearing the stinging hand of reality: Its freedom wavers
as that abandoned casing left atop the stage, beneath fading spotlight,
yearns for its partner, beckons,
twitches as the puppeteer cuts his strings.
An elastic band of will stretched too far, quivers under the strain;
its yearning fuels its strife, for reality beckons, fate awaits
and tensions snap! that wilful cord.
Away it drifts, further onto a path no legs can stride,
where its partner may not follow, for time has come up short,
and though they have shared much,
this is where reality and fantasy separate;
this is where body and soul end their embrace.
For hope cannot will the soul,
and the soul cannot hope to will.

It drifts away, taking the best of what it can,
and leaves its companion for journeys passed;
drifts, taking the solace of memories felt, known.
And this is when we finally live
along the solitary journey of the soul,
For this is when we part.
Close curtains.